Mike Holt's Illustrated Guide to

UNDERSTANDING
ELECTRICAL ESTIMATING

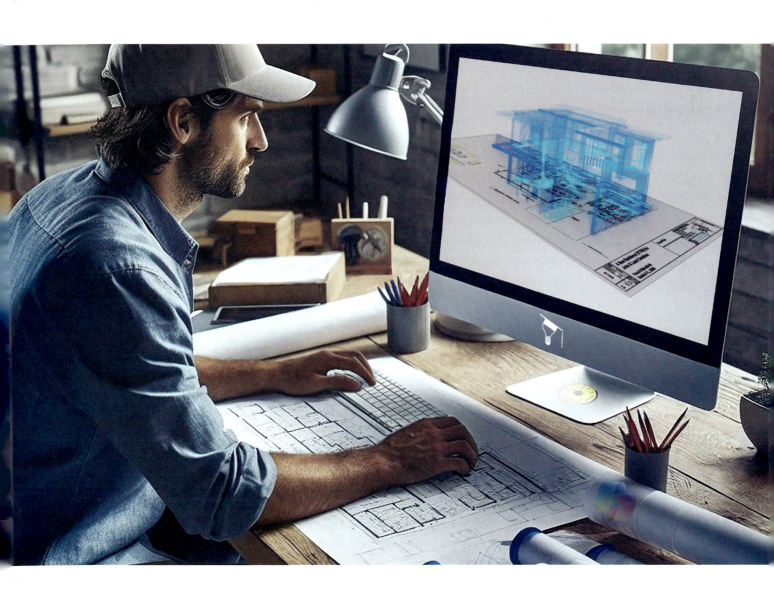

Mike Holt Enterprises
MikeHolt.com • 888.632.2633

NOTICE TO THE READER

Mike Holt's Illustrated Guide to Understanding Electrical Estimating

Second Printing: March 2025

Technical Illustrator: Mike Culbreath
Layout Design and Typesetting: Cathleen Kwas
Cover Design: Image generated with the assistance of Microsoft Copilot

COPYRIGHT © 2024 Charles Michael Holt
ISBN 978-1-960005-40-3

Produced and Printed in the USA

For more information, call 888.632.2633, or e-mail Info@MikeHolt.com.

This logo is a registered trademark of Mike Holt Enterprises, Inc.

If you are an instructor and would like to request an examination copy of this or other Mike Holt Publications:

Call: 888.632.2633 • Fax: 352.360.0983
E-mail: Info@MikeHolt.com • Visit: www.MikeHolt.com

You can download a sample PDF of all our publications by visiting www.MikeHolt.com

I dedicate this book to the
Lord Jesus Christ, *my mentor and teacher.*
Proverbs 16:3

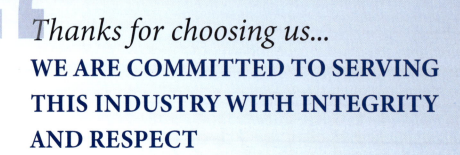

Thanks for choosing us...
WE ARE COMMITTED TO SERVING THIS INDUSTRY WITH INTEGRITY AND RESPECT

Since 1975, we have worked hard to develop products that get results, and to help individuals in their pursuit of success in this exciting industry.

From the very beginning we have been committed to the idea that customers come first. Everyone on my team will do everything they possibly can to help you succeed. I want you to know that we value you and are honored that you have chosen us to be your partner in training.

You are the future of this industry and we know that it is you who will make the difference in the years to come. My goal is to share with you everything that I know and to encourage you to pursue your education on a continuous basis. I hope that not only will you learn theory, *Code*, calculations, or how to pass an exam, but that in the process, you will become the expert in the field and the person others know to trust.

To put it simply, we genuinely care about your success and will do everything that we can to help you take your skills to the next level!

We are happy to partner with you on your educational journey.

God bless and much success,

TABLE OF CONTENTS

ABOUT THIS TEXTBOOK ix

Mike Holt's Illustrated Guide to Understanding Electrical Estimating x

Additional Products to Help You Learn xvi

CHAPTER 1—INTRODUCTION TO ESTIMATING 1

1.1 Introduction to Estimating 2

1.2 Who Needs an Estimate? 3

1.3 What Is an Estimate? 4

1.4 Estimate Types 6

1.5 Estimates and Design Stages 8

1.6 Estimating System 10

1.7 Estimating vs Bidding 12

1.8 Can I Be Competitive? 14

1.9 The Electrical Market 21

Final Thoughts 22

Chapter 1—Review Questions 23

CHAPTER 2—QUALITIES OF AN ESTIMATOR 35

2.1 Introduction..36

2.2 Personal Qualities of an Estimator 36

2.3 Responsibilities of an Estimator 37

2.4 Field Experience and Job Skills...41

Final Thoughts 42

Chapter 2—Review Questions 43

CHAPTER 3—THE ESTIMATING PROCESS 47

3.1   Introduction 48

3.2   The Estimating Workspace 48

3.3   The Estimating Tools 49

3.4   The Detailed Estimating Method 52

3.5   Estimate Accuracy 54

3.6   Estimating Techniques 56

       Final Thoughts 61

       Chapter 3—Review Questions 62

CHAPTER 4—THE TAKEOFF 69

4.1   Introduction 70

4.2   The Takeoff Sequence 70

4.3   The Takeoff 85

4.4   Takeoff Systems 90

4.5   Determining the Bill of Material 93

4.6   Determining Labor 96

4.7   Pricing Material and Labor 98

4.8   Extension 102

4.9   Historical Data 104

       Final Thoughts 104

       Chapter 4—Review Questions 105

CHAPTER 5—DETERMINING LABOR COSTS 113

5.1   Introduction 114

5.2   Basis of a Labor Unit 114

5.3   Expressing Labor Units 116

5.4   Components of a Labor Unit 120

5.5   Labor-Unit Manuals 123

5.6   Adjusting Labor Units 124

5.7   Labor Unit Variables 127

       Final Thoughts 143

       Chapter 5—Review Questions 144

Understanding Electrical Estimating | Mike Holt Enterprises

vi

CHAPTER 6—UNIT PRICING 153

6.1	Introduction	154
6.2	What Is Unit Pricing?	154
6.3	Unit Pricing Applications	155
	Final Thoughts	157
	Chapter 6—Review Questions	158

CHAPTER 7—DETERMINING BREAK-EVEN COST 161

7.1	Introduction	162
7.2	Break-Even Cost Summary Worksheet	163
7.3	Labor Hours and Labor Cost	164
7.4	Material Cost	176
7.5	Direct-Job Expenses	180
7.6	Estimated Prime Cost	184
7.7	Overhead	184
7.8	Break-Even Cost Review	188
	Final Thoughts	189
	Chapter 7—Review Questions	190

CHAPTER 8—THE BID PROCESS 197

8.1	Introduction	198
8.2	Listen to Your Gut Feelings	198
8.3	Job Selection	200
8.4	Financial Resources	201
8.5	Just Say No!	201
8.6	Understanding Bid Types	202
8.7	The Accurate Bid	205
8.8	How Much Profit Is Reasonable?	209
8.9	Calculating Bid Price	211
8.10	Bid Analysis	214
8.11	The Proposal	217
8.12	Closing the Deal	220
	Final Thoughts	221
	Chapter 8—Review Questions	222

Understanding Electrical Estimating | MikeHolt.com

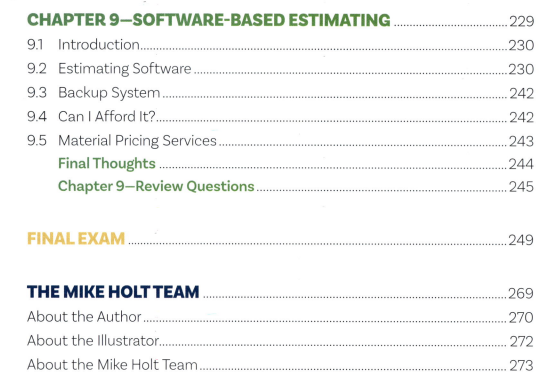

CHAPTER 9—SOFTWARE-BASED ESTIMATING 229

9.1   Introduction 230

9.2   Estimating Software 230

9.3   Backup System 242

9.4   Can I Afford It? 242

9.5   Material Pricing Services 243

     Final Thoughts 244

     Chapter 9—Review Questions 245

FINAL EXAM 249

THE MIKE HOLT TEAM 269

About the Author 270

About the Illustrator 272

About the Mike Holt Team 273

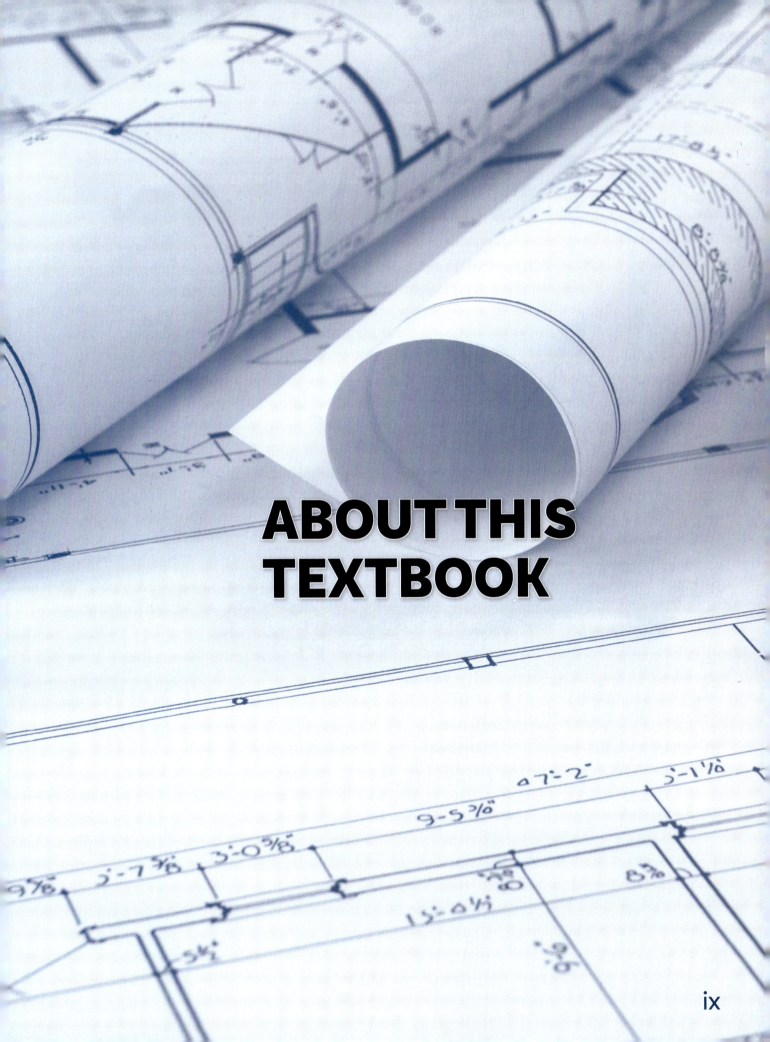

ABOUT THIS TEXTBOOK

Mike Holt's Illustrated Guide to Understanding Electrical Estimating

Congratulations on making the decision to learn about electrical estimating. This is a skill set that can make or break your career, and may make or break a company. Creating an accurate estimate isn't just making "an educated guess." Estimating is a methodology with precise requirements that helps you to consistently produce an accurate projection of project costs. With some practice, you can learn the skills and techniques that will allow you to produce a high quality estimate in a timely manner that will allow your company to accurately predict material and labor needs so you can successfully and consistently manage your project for a profit!

While today most people use electrical estimating software to create estimates, you need to understand the numbers and the process behind the estimate if you want to stay in business. The often-quoted Francis Bacon said "knowledge is power." That couldn't be more true in the business realm, and an accurate estimate is often the source of that knowledge.

The following is a list of ways an accurate estimate helps a business have the knowledge it needs to be successful:

- It allows you to create an accurate cost for a project.
- You will be able to meet the customer's specifications with confidence.
- The project management team can use that estimate as a budget plan to manage projects profitably.
- Materials can be ordered based on the estimate, to keep work flowing without stockpiling costly materials "just in case."
- Cash flow can be managed in a proactive manner to avoid shortfalls. As we all know, cash flow is the lifeblood of every company.

To get these benefits, you must understand the concepts behind making an accurate estimate and what the methods are for arriving at the correct final numbers. This course is designed to help you understand all these concepts, and more.

By completing this course, you will begin to understand that estimating is a way of seeing, in advance, what it will take to complete a given project on time and within budget for a happy customer and a *profitable bottom line*.

Many variables figure into an estimate that may easily be missed or forgotten. However, a methodical approach to estimating will include those variables, allowing the project estimator to:

- avoid unexpected costs after the project is already underway
- determine manpower needs
- determine if your workforce is properly skilled to complete the work
- determine overall if the project is a good fit for your company

You can't do every job that comes along, nor would you want to. With accurate estimates, you can bid on those projects that are the best fit for your company's resources and are the most profitable.

Estimating Program Focus

The topic of estimating is one that is surrounded with mystery and drama. All too often people are not educated on the simple principles of estimating and cost themselves, or their company, huge amounts of money. Our goal is to expose you to the principles that lay beneath a solid estimating process so you can understand what estimating is and how to do it right. There are many variables in the documents used to produce an estimate. For simplicity, this program is based on estimating jobs with a set of construction drawings. As you progress in your career you will find that even specialty work and service calls can use many of the same principles that are discussed in this course regardless of the types of documents that are being provided at the time of the estimate.

Understanding Electrical Estimating | MikeHolt.com

Scope of This Textbook

The primary purpose of this text is to help you understand the estimating and bidding processes. We will explain how to determine material cost, labor cost, and the calculation of direct job costs, overhead, and profit to complete the bid. As you learn about estimating, you will get a light review of some basic business principles so you can understand estimating. If you struggle in these areas make sure to check out our Business Management Skills library so you can take full advantage of having an accurate estimate.

Mike Holt's *Illustrated Guide to Understanding Electrical Estimating* is divided into 9 chapters.

Chapter 1—Introduction to Estimating. Chapter 1 explains what estimating is, and the purpose, importance, and need for proper estimating.

Chapter 2—Qualities of an Estimator. This chapter explains the qualities and responsibilities of a good estimator.

Chapter 3—The Estimating Process. This chapter discusses the importance of a properly equipped and organized estimating space, the tools of the estimating trade, and the basics of the detailed estimating method.

Chapter 4—The Takeoff. In this chapter we will discuss both the science and the art of the takeoff including some common methods used to ensure an accurate count when reviewing drawings.

Chapter 5—Determining Labor Costs. This chapter will give you a detailed description of what labor units are, how they work, and when to use them. Knowing the cost of labor is a key component of an accurate estimate.

Chapter 6—Unit Pricing. Sometimes, when estimating large numbers of repetitive tasks, unit price estimating can be accurate and a huge time saver. This chapter introduces this concept and explains the pros and cons of estimating with unit prices.

Chapter 7—Determining Break-Even Cost. To know how much money you will make on a project, you have to know what it will cost you to do the job. In estimating this is called the "Break-Even-Cost."

Chapter 8—The Bid Process. Once you have determined the cost of a job, you have to figure out how to sell the job for a profit. This is called the bid process. In Chapter 8, you'll learn how to make an educated decision about when and where to spend your time and money. You need to make this decision early in the estimating process so that you don't waste time producing a bid for a job you shouldn't take.

Chapter 9—Software-Based Estimating. Chapter 9 will give you an overview of how to use technology to become a better estimator. It is important to remember that estimating software is a tool and cannot by itself ensure your success. It will, however, allow estimators to improve accuracy, consistency, and speed when preparing estimates.

Answer Keys

 Digital answer keys are included with all purchases of Mike Holt book orders, and can be found in your online account at Mike Holt Enterprises. Go to MikeHolt.com/MyAccount and log in to your account, or create one if you haven't already done so. If you are not currently a Mike Holt customer, you can access your answer key at MikeHolt.com/MyAKEST.

Watch the Videos That Accompany This Textbook

Brian House, along with an expert panel, recorded videos to accompany this textbook. Watching these videos will provide context for each of the sections of the text, along with explanations and additional commentary that expand on the topics. Brian and the panel discuss the nuances behind estimating, and cover their practical application in the real world.

 To watch sample video clips from this program, scan this QR Code or visit MikeHolt.com/ESTvideos. To get the complete video library for this book, call 888.632.2633 to find out how to upgrade your program or visit MikeHolt.com/UpgradeEST.

Note: Estimating forms and practice plans for commercial, multi-family, residential and restaurants will be available for free if you upgrade to the video package, and are included with the purchase of the Understanding Electrical Estimating Video Library.

Technical Questions

As you progress through this textbook, you might find that you don't understand every explanation, example, calculation, or comment. If you find some topics difficult to understand, even after watching the videos, we recommend you discuss your questions with instructors, co-workers, or other students—they might have a perspective that will help you understand more clearly.

 If you have additional questions that aren't covered in this material, visit MikeHolt.com/Forum, and post your question.

Textbook Errors and Corrections

We're committed to providing you the finest product with the fewest errors and take great care to ensure our textbooks are correct. But we're realistic and know that errors might be found after printing. If you believe that there's an error of any kind (typographical, grammatical, technical, etc.) in this textbook or in the Answer Key, please visit MikeHolt.com/Corrections and complete the online Textbook Correction Form.

Key Features

The layout and design of this textbook incorporate special features and symbols designed to help you navigate easily through the material.

Electrical Plans
Electrical drawings, legends and plans illustrate the concepts.

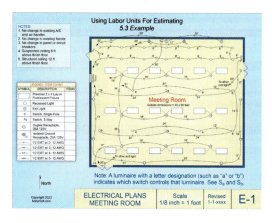

Word of Caution

These icons highlight areas of concern or words of advice.

Word of Caution: Be careful not to make a mistake when transferring the supplier's prices to your summary worksheet. Insist on written quotes and be sure the quote includes any freight and shipping costs.

Tips

These practical suggestions and words of advice can help you save time or work more efficiently and accurately.

If you bid on a job at a theme park or beach, you should increase the labor requirements for distractions!

Comments

Observations from the author's years of experience.

Remember—there isn't a set of labor units that fits every job.

Formulas

Formulas are easily identifiable in green text on a gray bar.

Job Days = Total Job Hours/Hours Worked per Day

Case Studies

These samples provide results of real-world scenarios.

Case Study No. 1: A friend of mine, who was just getting started in business, did not read the note on the drawing that required him to replace 180 ft of 4/0 AWG service conductors with 500 kcmil service conductors.

The Result: He underbid the job by $4,000 on a $35,000 job and won the job losing $4,000!

Examples

Practical application examples are contained in framed yellow boxes.

>
>
> **Labor Cost Example:** The total adjusted estimated labor is 109.77 hours and the labor rate per man-hour is $18.00.
>
> **Estimated Labor Cost = Total Adjusted Estimated Labor Hours × Labor Rate per Man-Hour**
> Estimated Labor Cost = 109.77 hours × $18.00
> Estimated Labor Cost = $1,975.86

Additional Products to Help You Learn

Upgrade Your Textbook with the Understanding Electrical Estimating Videos

One of the best ways to get the most out of this textbook is to use it in conjunction with the corresponding videos, which feature a panel of industry specialists. The videos showcase dynamic discussions, analysis of the topics, explanation of the nuances, and the application of estimating in the field. Upgrade your program today!

UPGRADE PACKAGE INCLUDES:

- *Understanding Electrical Estimating videos*
- *Estimating practice forms and plans*

Digital answer key

Plus! A digital version of the textbook

Product Code: [ESTUPGRADEVI]

 Ready to get started? To add the videos that accompany this textbook, call our office at 888.632.2633 to find out how to upgrade your product, scan the QR code or visit MikeHolt.com/UpgradeEST.

Have questions? E-mail Info@MikeHolt.com.

Understanding Electrical Estimating | Mike Holt Enterprises

2nd Printing

Understanding Electrical Theory, for *NEC* Applications, Video Program

Whether you're a first-year apprentice still struggling to understand the difference between a volt or ampere, or a veteran trying to sharpen your troubleshooting skills, this product has something for you. Once you know the principles behind how electricity works, you will be ready to correctly apply the rules in the *National Electrical Code®* (*NEC®*) to the work you do every day.

This video program will take you on a journey that begins with the physics behind how electricity works, all the way through topics and concepts that are relevant to everyone working in the electrical industry.

PROGRAM INCLUDES:

Understanding Electrical Theory for *NEC* Applications Textbook

- *Electrical Theory videos*

Digital answer keys

Plus! A digital version of the textbook

Product Code: [THLIBMM]

 To order, visit MikeHolt.com/Theory, call 888.632.2633, or scan the QR code

Understanding the *NEC* Complete Video Library

How well do you know the *Code*? When you really need to understand the *NEC*, there's no better way to learn it than with Mike's *NEC* Complete Training Library. This program has helped thousands of electricians master technical concepts and feel confident using their *Code* book. The lessons take you step-by-step through the *National Electrical Code* with detailed illustrations, great practice questions, author's comments, and in-depth analysis. Mike guides you through the most utilized rules and breaks them down so you can understand the rule as well as how to apply it in the field.

This library is perfect for engineers, electricians, contractors, and electrical inspectors

PROGRAM* INCLUDES:

Understanding the *National Electrical Code*—Volume 1 Textbook
- *Understanding the NEC Volume 1 videos*

Understanding the *National Electrical Code*—Volume 2 Textbook
- *Understanding the NEC Volume 2 videos*

Bonding and Grounding Textbook
- *Bonding and Grounding videos*

Fundamental *NEC* Calculations Textbook
- *Fundamental NEC Calculations videos*

Understanding the *National Electrical Code* Workbook (Articles 90-480)

Digital answer keys

Plus! A digital version of each book

Product Code: [UNDLIBMM]

Description based on the 2023 NEC edition of this product

To order, visit MikeHolt.com/Code, call 888.632.2633, or scan the QR code

Mike Holt's Leadership and Life Skills Video Program

In this program, Mike shares his insight and knowledge of the skills and disciplines you need in order to understand who you are, make goals, and work to achieve them. Continuous improvement is necessary to learn how to embrace change, conflict, and failure. Whatever your current position or goals, you'll learn tips and processes that will help you raise your game.

Leadership. Leadership has to do with the day-to-day choices you make to succeed in your personal life or in your work. Mike shows you how to develop and improve on the skills that will help you become a successful player in your own life and be in control of your own destiny—whatever you determine that to be.

Life Skills. Learn with Mike as he shares his wisdom and experiences that have made him successful in life and in business. He gives you the tools to clear the path to understand what success looks like to you, how to cultivate a winning attitude, and how to employ great communications skills.

PROGRAM INCLUDES:

Leadership Skills Textbook

Life Skills Workbook

- *Life Skills videos and streaming audio*

Plus! A digital version of each book

Product Code: [LEADMM]

To order, visit MikeHolt.com/Life, call 888.632.2633, or scan the QR code.

Notes...

2nd Printing

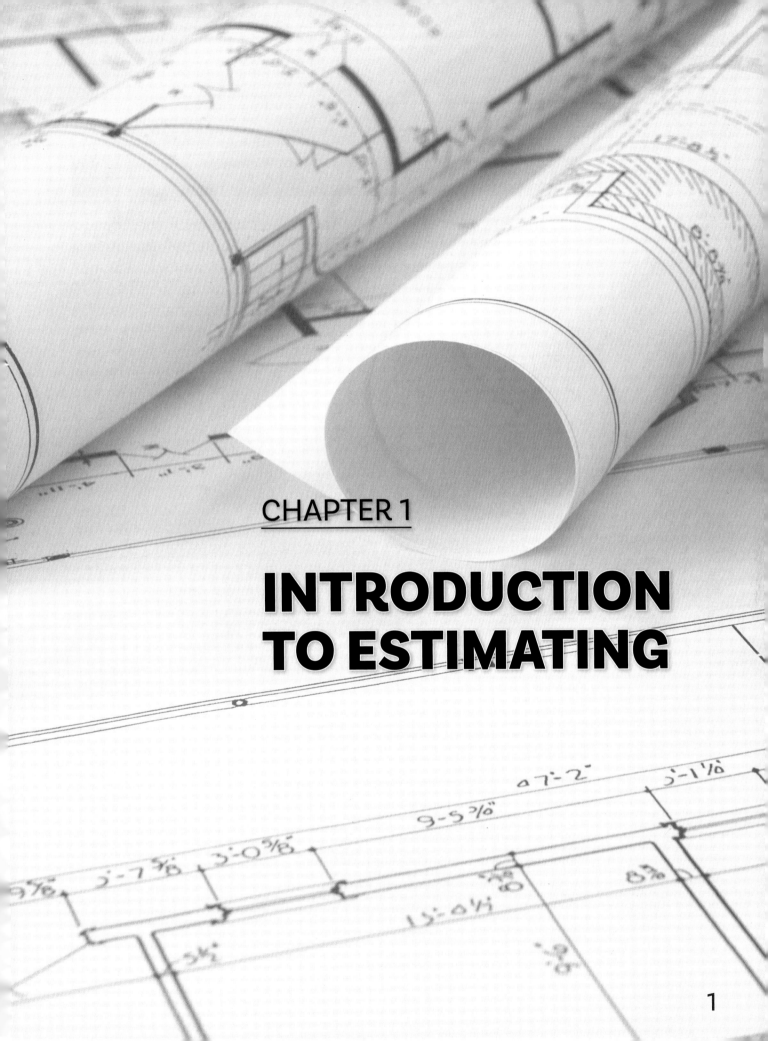

CHAPTER 1

INTRODUCTION TO ESTIMATING

1

1.1 Introduction to Estimating

An estimate in its simplest form is a calculation of the cost to complete a specific amount of work under a set of conditions. Estimates are often used by a contractor to create a bid price that can be submitted to a soliciting contractor or owner who needs a price for work on a project. However, estimates are also used for internal business management purposes such as qualifying jobs, creating unit prices, determining the feasibility of projects for your company, and for business projections to achieve maximum profit while maintaining cash flow.

Most electrical construction and maintenance work is obtained through a bidding process where multiple contractors submit a bid price to the customer. The customer then chooses the bid with a scope of work and price that best suits their needs.

To create a bid, a contractor uses the cost estimate to calculate the type and amount of work the customer has requested based on project documents like plans, drawings, or specifications. To determine the selling price to the customer, the contractor uses the estimate information to produce a bid price based on risk and the desired amount of profit.

This chapter lays the foundation for your understanding of the process of creating electrical estimates for the purpose of determining the bid price, which is covered in Chapter 8. It also introduces how estimates are used in the bid process and is organized in the following way:

1.2   Who Needs an Estimate?

1.3   What Is an Estimate?

1.4   Estimate Types

1.5   Estimates and Design Stages

1.6   Estimating System

1.7   Estimating vs Bidding

1.8   Can I Be Competitive?

1.9   The Electrical Market

2nd Printing

1.2 Who Needs an Estimate?

As you begin this journey you might be wondering who needs an estimate. The short answer is almost every person that is in business needs an estimate of cost for some type of work or service so they can make sound financial decisions.

Electrical contractors are no exception to this, and in many cases creating estimates is a part of their daily life. Most electrical contractors wear many hats such as estimator, project manager, secretary, warehouse person, truck driver, supervisor, electrician, salesperson, CEO, finance officer, credit manager, and so on. There are not enough hours in the day or night for any one person to keep up with all these demands, so eventually something starts to slip, and it's usually the things that take the most time and require the most focus.

Since creating an estimate takes time and focus, it is often relegated to the late evening hours, and is one of the first things that gets rushed. This leads to an inaccurate estimate leaving no way to correctly determine project costs. The likelihood that the estimate will be accurate when you are tired, distracted, and under pressure is very low.

If you do not know the cost of a project, you're unlikely to stay in business very long. Your bids will either be so high that you don't get much work, or so low, that you get a lot of work, lose money on every job, and eventually go out of business.

While there is no single thing that can ensure you will be successful in business, one big step in the right direction is to know what it costs to complete your projects so that you can submit a successful bid and use the estimate to manage the project for sufficient profit.

Understanding Electrical Estimating | MikeHolt.com

Contractor Success

All businesses exist for one reason and that is to make money (profit)! So, while you may enjoy your work (and I hope you do) or are even passionate about it (and I hope you are), the purpose of an electrical contractor is to make a profit on every single job.

Profit is a reward for taking risks, so it is important to be aware of, and evaluate, the degree of risk contained in each job. Providing the best service, with the most profit possible while remaining competitive, is essential to being successful as a contractor

As of 2022, there were over 75,000 electrical contractors in the United States competing for $225 billion worth of work, making competition fierce. The successful electrical contractor must accurately estimate costs, successfully bid, and competently manage projects so they can compete profitably in a highly competitive marketplace.

1.3 What Is an Estimate?

Estimating is the process used to calculate the cost to complete a certain type and amount of work. An estimate is a document that contains the details of these costs.

Purpose

The purpose of estimating is to determine the cost of a project before you do the work. The estimate must consider the following factors:

- Job conditions
- Cost of materials
- Labor cost
- Labor availability
- Job expenses, risks, and overhead

Direct and Indirect Costs

An accurate estimate is calculated by including costs for the following:

- Equipment and services
- Labor
- Material

These costs can be either directly related to the completion of the work that is being estimated (direct costs), or they may be costs that are incurred because the business exists, but are not directly related to a specific job (indirect costs). In both cases estimating accounts for these costs, so that they can be included in the selling price of work to ensure the profitability of the business.

Direct Costs

Direct costs are a component of job cost. They include items that are expenses that have been incurred specifically because the job was taken on. Direct costs do not include costs that would be incurred in the normal course of business operation. Examples of direct costs include:

- Material
- Sales tax
- Subcontract cost
- Rental expenses
- Job overhead and labor

Indirect Cost

Indirect costs are not a part of the costs incurred to complete a specific job. They are general expenses that are a normal part of operating the business. Indirect costs include employee benefits, business operational overhead, and management expenses.

Understanding Electrical Estimating | MikeHolt.com

Profit

You might be wondering why profit isn't included in this list. That is because profit is added to the estimated total as the final step before submitting the bid. Profit is not a part of determining how much it costs to do the job, but rather a step in determining how much to sell a job for. The topic of profit is covered more in later chapters.

1.4 Estimate Types

The purpose of estimating is to determine the cost of a project before you actually do the work. Estimating must take into consideration variable job conditions, material costs, labor costs, labor availability, direct-job expenses, risks, and management costs (overhead).

Estimates can be divided into three basic types:

- Preliminary or Budget Estimate
- Quantity or Piece-Rate Estimate
- Detailed Estimate

Preliminary or Budget Estimate

The preliminary or budget estimate is for budgeting purposes and is usually completed before plans are drawn up. It's generally based on:

- The description of the use of the facility
- The square-foot dimensions
- How the facility will be used
- The proposed type of construction

The preliminary or budget estimate provides the estimated cost, along with a projected profit and overhead number, during the design phase to determine the feasibility of the project. Preliminary or budget estimates may be utilized internally, or they may be provided to the customer/contractor with a negotiated profit and overhead rate, to allow the contract manager to provide pricing to the consumer based on demand.

> **Word of Caution:** Preliminary budget bids should only be for someone with whom you have a relationship and who you would do the work for normally. Providing budget bids can be a complete waste of time as there is an extremely low likelihood of conversion to paid work. In addition, the contract award price will never be based on who provided a design number.

Quantity or Piece-Rate Estimate

Quantity or piece-rate estimates are common in several sectors of the electrical industry. This type of estimate is used for:

- Repetitive work with no variety
- Internal analysis
- Negotiated profit and overhead contracts
- Itemized work in which variable costs can be billed separately

Quantity or piece-rate estimates may be utilized internally, or they may be provided to the customer/contractor with a negotiated profit and overhead rate to allow the contract manager to provide pricing to the consumer based on demand.

An example of a quantity or piece-rate estimate would be one that determines the cost to install 500 job trailers at various locations. Separate fixed prices might be provided to set a power pole, hook up the trailer, install a light pole light, and so on. Other costs and expenses such as travel and permitting, which can vary greatly, are often billed separately to allow the budget for the project to be easily managed. This avoids redundant administrative work for the parts of the work that don't change from job to job.

Word of Caution: Be careful if you get involved in this type of work. A little mistake can turn into a huge one when it is multiplied by the total number of units that you commit to build.

Detailed Estimate

The detailed estimate is what most electrical contractors think of when they say the word estimate. The detailed estimate is an itemized list of labor and materials based on plans and/or specifications. This is the most accurate type of estimate and is used for almost every type of work. A detailed estimate contains the information you need to make money!

1.5 Estimates and Design Stages

Estimates are used to determine the cost of a project once the design has been established. That said, there are several different stages of design and an estimate can be required in any or all of them for a given project. The quality of the design documents is the most important single factor affecting the estimated cost, so it's important to understand what types of documents there are and the kind of estimate they can produce.

The design drawings stages include:

- Schematic Drawings
- Design Development Drawings
- Construction Drawings
- No Drawings

Schematic Drawings

Schematic drawings are very general conceptual drawings and they:

- Contain a basic floorplan and elevations
- Are used for job budgets
- Are unsuitable for contract documents

Design Development Drawings

These drawings are often called the "DDs," and are approximately 50-60 percent complete. They are still conceptual drawings but missing the higher level of details and specifications found in construction drawings.

While these should never be used as contract documents, the practice in the field is often to go to contract with these documents and make the subcontractor "figure it out." Never submit a bid price unless you have a 100 percent complete set of drawings. If you do, carefully document anything that wasn't clear in the drawings.

Construction Drawings

Construction drawings are the final stage of design drawings. These are ready to be built with minimal deviation from the printed drawing. You often won't receive these until after you are awarded a contract. It's *critical* that your estimate contains enough detail to easily identify what has changed between the bid set and the construction set. If there is a cost impact on your scope of work, you may need to write a few change orders before the job starts.

No Drawings

There is a fourth scenario that electrical contractors are regularly called upon to engage in, and that is producing an estimate when there are no drawings at all. This mainly happens when an owner calls for minor alterations to an existing building or, more commonly, for

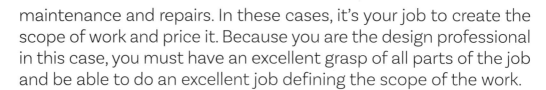

maintenance and repairs. In these cases, it's your job to create the scope of work and price it. Because you are the design professional in this case, you must have an excellent grasp of all parts of the job and be able to do an excellent job defining the scope of the work.

For the purposes of this material, we'll focus on estimating jobs having construction drawings as they contain all the steps necessary for any type of estimate. Just remember, no matter what type of estimate you do, accuracy in the estimating phase can be your salvation when you get into a difficult situation during a project.

1.6 Estimating System

An estimating system is a set of tools that help you quickly and accurately determine the cost of a project that includes *all* anticipated costs.

When the term "estimating system" is used, the common misconception is that it refers to a piece of software. That couldn't be further from the truth. To be efficient and accurate, it must be systematic to keep errors to a minimum.

An estimating system is made up of several components including checklists of required documents, proper software, or conventional takeoff and measuring tools, spreadsheets, and reference materials. As you complete this material, you will learn what these tools are and when you need to use them to produce a good estimate.

Estimates are used for the following:

- Project Management
- Project Budget
- Material Management
- Labor Management
- Adjustments

Understanding Electrical Estimating | Mike Holt Enterprises

Project Management

Successful contractors survive because they know how to use an estimate as a tool to help manage costs and ensure the targeted amount of profit is made.

Proper project management makes the difference between profit and loss for an accurately estimated project. For the highest chance of project management success, a project budget should be created by the estimating system and communicated to the project team by the estimator.

Project Budget

The project budget is based on the estimate. The budget describes the material and labor required for each phase of the job and when the material and labor will be needed.

Material Management

One of the important functions of the project budget is material management. A proper project budget tells the construction team what types and quantities of materials and tools are needed and when they are needed. Without a good estimate to predict material and tool needs, you won't have what you need when you need it. This will result in poor field performance and reduced profit.

Labor Management

The *largest* risk on a project is labor cost. The labor estimate is the tool used to determine when and how much labor is required for the job. Proper project labor scheduling is the fastest way to increase efficiency and profit. Too little manpower on the job can create conflicts with other trades and the owner because you are behind. Too much manpower at the wrong time will frustrate superintendents, lower productivity, and increase costs!

Understanding Electrical Estimating | MikeHolt.com

Adjustments

Adjusting the project budget (estimate) as a job progresses is often required due to employee productivity and site conditions. Ensure you have a system in place to collect feedback from the jobsite and record it in the estimating system for future reference.

1.7 Estimating vs Bidding

A common mistake in the construction trade is to confuse or interchange the terms estimate and bid. As we just discussed, the estimate is used to calculate the cost of a project, but if the work is going to be sold, we need to create a selling price for that work called a bid price. The bid is presented to the owner or soliciting contractor for approval and represents the amount of compensation the contractor expects for the work being performed.

The bid price is calculated by adding profit to the estimated cost of the job. This total is the price that the customer will pay for the work that will be performed.

There are three basic bid types that are used to communicate the bid price of a job to the customer:

Bid Types

- Competitive Bids
- Negotiated Bids
- Best Value Bids

Competitive Bids

Competitive bid work requires the contractor to submit a price, or a set of prices, which will be charged to perform the services required in accordance with the drawings and specifications. This bid process requires competing contractors to submit bids, and the customer chooses from among them.

2nd Printing

Negotiated Bids

Negotiated bids are used when the electrical contractor works directly with the customer to negotiate a price based on the customer's needs.

To negotiate bids, you need:

- Cost of the project (estimate)
- Confidence in your bid price
- Relationship with the customer

> **Word of Caution:** Never go into a negotiation without an estimate. Things may sound doable at the time, but once you "work up the numbers," you may discover that you've just set your company up for cascading cash-flow problems, resource conflicts, or even failure to perform.

Negotiated bids require a long-term relationship with the customer or vendor. They must know that you are honest, professional, and provide quality service. This type of relationship creates an opportunity to negotiate the price. A negotiated bid avoids competing to be the low bidder, but you *need* to know your cost, which means you *need* an estimate.

Best Value Bids

Sometimes, the goal is to show the value you bring to your customer to support the bid you submitted. Often this is referred to as a best value bid. This type of bid relies on alternate installation methods, gear packages, and fixture packages to be more cost-effective. You must have a rapport with the customer, or they will not feel safe choosing a value-engineered bid.

1.8 Can I Be Competitive?

In the world of business, it's never about how competitive your price is, it's about being profitable on a job because you have an accurate estimate that can be used to project costs and manage the job well. This will reduce waste and allow you to achieve adequate profit at a lower selling price. The following factors can all impact your ability to be profitable at a competitive price:

- The Market
- Management Skills
- Experience
- Risk vs Reward
- Labor Costs and Productivity
- Wages
- Other Bidders
- Cost of Material (Buying Power)
- Overhead

The Market

Many factors will determine if you can be competitive. The most significant factor is the condition of the market and the amount of available work.

In a robust market where the supply of work exceeds available contractors, it's easy to make money because you can win a bid at higher than normal prices, which allows for significant inefficiency while still returning a profit.

During a tight market, it's more difficult to win jobs because of the increase in competition. Try to focus on your area of expertise rather than bidding on jobs where you have no experience—this will allow you to be your most competitive.

Most electrical contractors are concerned about their ability to be competitive, make money, and stay in business. To be competitive and profitable, you must offer the customer a quality service at a reasonable price. To accomplish this, the electrical contractor must control the job and administrative (overhead) costs, so they are within the estimated budget.

Management Skills

Successful electrical contractors know how to manage their labor and material in accordance with the estimate. Many electrical contractors are electricians without formal business management training; as a result, they might not do a very good job as business owners.

To be successful, you need to attend management seminars, watch training videos, and become involved with a local contractors' organization to learn from the mistakes of others.

Many electrical contractors do not realize that they are not alone in their experiences. Consider joining an electrical contractors' organization where you can learn from the experience of those who have been there before you. Learning from another contractor's misfortune is always better than making the mistake yourself.

Joining an organization that provides you with the training and insight you need to be successful will reduce your stress levels and give you a better opportunity to avoid a big mistake.

Experience

The more experience your company has with a given type of construction, the more efficient and productive similar jobs will be. This means you will be able to do the job with less labor time, resulting in a reduction in the estimated cost. Each job carries a degree of risk which can be affected by the amount of experience you have with that type of job.

Understanding Electrical Estimating | MikeHolt.com

To gain the experience you need to be competitive in an unfamiliar market, educate yourself by attending seminars, reading trade magazines, and watching training videos. Do whatever you can to minimize your inexperience but expect the labor cost for the first few jobs in a new market to be higher than subsequent jobs.

> **Word of Caution:** An uneducated or unethical contractor is the biggest hindrance to obtaining a fair price for your work. Avoid them!

Risk vs Reward

Risk must be considered when putting together an estimate for an unfamiliar type of work. The greater the perceived risk, the higher the profit margin (reward) needs to be to offset possible losses. As you gain experience, your profit margin percentage can be higher, and your bid will be more competitive because you don't need to include extra padding for the unknown.

> When you submit a bid and are not awarded the job, ask the customer for a briefing to review your costs and technical approach. This will help build valuable estimating knowledge for a particular type of work and customer, so you are more competitive on future bids.

Labor Costs and Productivity

Labor costs can be a huge factor in your ability to be competitive. Competitiveness between contractors based on different pay scales can be significant; some pay rock-bottom wages and others pay union scale. Hire and retain highly skilled, motivated, and educated employees. Even if the pay rate is higher, the efficiency of the team will easily offset the loss and stress of using unskilled employees.

Wages

Create a pay scale that encourages productivity and education. Pay your team based on what they can produce—not what's on the market. Their salary should compensate them for their abilities and their contribution to your company's bottom line. By paying top dollar and giving benefits, you should be able to hire and retain highly skilled, motivated, and educated electricians to work for you for years, if not a lifetime.

> I have many employees that have been with me for 20, 30 years, as a result of this philosophy.

It is not necessary to pay all electricians the same wage. Higher skilled electricians earn the company more and *should* be paid more. They also motivate and help the lesser skilled to become more skilled.

Having motivated, loyal, and skilled electricians who have been with your organization for years will ultimately result in a lower labor installation cost as opposed to having an unhappy and unskilled labor force who feel no loyalty to your company. If you pay low wages, you can expect problems with your employees, the inspector, general contractors, and other trades. This all spills over into the customer's experience with your company—and your bottom line.

Remember, your employees are the people who represent your company and interface directly with your customers. You must keep them happy!

Other Bidders

Make it a point to know your competition. Consider the number of contractors bidding on the job before you commit valuable time and energy to completing an estimate. When possible:

- Don't bid jobs with more than a few competitors
- Know your competition's capacity
- Monitor how busy your competitors are

Understanding Electrical Estimating | MikeHolt.com

Smaller-sized contractors have a few unique advantages that you must consider, so you understand the challenges *and* the opportunities that may exist when bidding.

Here are a few things to remember about small contractors:

- They might not be as price competitive as larger contractors
- They often have poor management skills
- They usually have narrower focus and more personalized service
- They can usually adapt to market changes quickly

If you're a smaller-sized contractor and you want to get more work, get the bid done immediately. The customer will see that you value them and their job and will be more likely to select you for the work.

Cost of Material (Buying Power)

Suppliers seldom acknowledge it, but they offer different prices to different contractors for the same material. To be offered the best price, become a good customer so it's in the suppliers' best interest to give you the best price.

A few simple rules for receiving the best price include:

- Pay your bills on time to take advantage of any discounts offered. Some suppliers will give their best-paying contractors lower prices.
- Be a partner, not a difficult customer. Suppliers want to make easy money, not deal with someone who is always trying to "get them."

Did you know that it costs more to pick your material up at the supply house counter than it does to have it delivered? Do not pick up your material if you have the option of having it delivered.

You should check with the supplier to be sure that the cost will be the same but realize that you must cover the cost of lost productivity and labor when material is picked up as opposed to having it delivered.

Another method to reduce material costs is to purchase commodity items in large quantities to obtain a lower price. It's important to weigh the cost of financing, storage, and double handling against the price advantage.

The lowest price is not everything; you will want a relationship with a supplier who will help you solve your problems, and who will be there when needed. Always remember the big picture—just like you want your customers to do.

Overhead

Overhead expenses are the costs incurred to operate the business. Examples are telephone expenses, shop rent, vehicles, advertising, insurance, office personnel, and so on. Overhead costs represent between 20 and 40 percent of an electrical contractor's total sales. It's critical to keep those costs as low as possible so you can keep a competitive edge.

Profit and Selling Price

Profit

As we have already discussed, profit is what ensures the success of your company. While profit is the primary goal, it isn't exclusive from all the other factors that will make you successful. Make sure you are careful to be profitable and at the same time always be sensitive to provide a quality product and a fair price to the customer. This will ensure that your success is long term and not just a flash in the pan.

Selling Price

Confidence and professionalism are important ingredients in getting your price. Confidence comes from knowing your price is a good value to the customer and that they will be pleased with the quality of service you provide.

Next to confidence is professionalism. Do you come across as a professional by your appearance and the appearance of your workers and vehicles? Many electrical contractors dress and carry themselves as a trades person rather than a businessperson.

When you are meeting with the customer, dress as a businessperson. But it does not stop there; ensure that your electricians and vehicles have a professional appearance. If you provide outstanding service at a reasonable price, you will close more contracts if you come across as a professional business organization.

Remember that not all customers are the same. Some customers want quality installation at a fair price, while others are willing to accept an inferior job as long as the price is low. With proper management, you can provide quality installation at a fair price, which will be more cost-effective in the long run for your customers, and better for your reputation.

The Loser

Being competitive doesn't mean that you will always win. In fact, if you are always winning you aren't competitive, you are just too low and risk putting yourself out of business! If you don't win the job, ask the customer to review your costs and technical approach. This will help you understand where you can adjust the next time you put together an estimate for this type of work. Don't be discouraged if you just can't get your number low enough. Often the winner of a bid is the one that made the biggest mistake on the estimate. Be glad that wasn't you! If you only remember one thing from this chapter, it should be that making money is more important than winning jobs.

> **TIP!**
>
> Never change your price or compromise your profit to chase work. All jobs are an unknown risk until you are done and have been paid. If you don't win a job, figure out why and revise your strategy for the future.

1.9 The Electrical Market

The electrical market is a dynamic and changing animal. It has opportunities for every type of business, from the high-volume contractor who focuses on production, to the niche contractor who has carved out a specific sector of the market to specialize in. It's important to be aware of the benefits and the risks of niche contracting as you consider the types of work that you want to estimate.

Niche Contractors

Many contractors develop a niche (a special place) in the market such as service, housing, medical facilities, banking, commercial buildings, or industrial maintenance. These niches require special knowledge and expertise and are a great place to make higher than usual profit margins, but they also carry some risk when they become the sole source of your business income. Make sure you are always careful to balance the work you take on to protect your income in the long term.

Word of Caution: The electrical industry is in constant change—parts of the market are expanding or contracting depending on technology, the economy, and customers' needs. So be careful, do not put all of your eggs in one basket or you might find your niche almost disappearing, as happened when the housing market collapsed in 2007.

Understanding Electrical Estimating | MikeHolt.com

Opportunities

New and expanding markets offer greater opportunities to develop new customers, possibly with fewer competitors and greater profit margins. Consider every bid request as an opportunity to monitor the market's direction, and then decide which path you'll choose to follow.

Final Thoughts

A large percentage of electrical companies obtain most of their electrical construction and maintenance work through the process of estimating and submitting bids, and the price must be based on a solid estimate. A correct estimate determines what it will cost you to complete the job according to the customer's needs, as described in the drawings and specifications. Electrical contractors are awarded most of their work through either competitive or negotiated bidding.

One of the most important things you have learned in this chapter is the purpose of electrical contracting. It is a business... and businesses exist to make money! That does not mean charging the most you can get by with or cheating customers, because companies that do such things tend not to be around for very long.

It means charging the correct prices and doing the work the right way so you can justify those prices. Many electrical contractors are unsuccessful because their prices are wrong. The solution is not merely to raise prices or to lower them. You have to charge the "right" price, and to do that you need to know what it costs to do a given job—that is where estimating comes in.

A good estimate is the foundation for a good bid and the budget needed to properly manage the job.

Use the information you learned in this chapter to answer the following questions.

Chapter 1—Review Questions

1.1 Introduction

1. Estimate information is used to produce a bid that considers risk and the ____ to determine the selling price to the customer.

    (a)   taxes
    (b)   desired profit
    (c)   insurance costs
    (d)   working height(s)

1.2 Who Needs an Estimate?

2. While there is no single thing that can ensure you will be successful in business, one big step in the right direction is to know what it costs to complete your projects and manage them ____.

    (a)   for sufficient profit
    (b)   for longevity
    (c)   skillfully
    (d)   to stay busy

3. Profit is a reward for taking risks, so it is important to be aware of and evaluate the ____ each job.

    (a)   travel time for
    (b)   skillset(s) required for
    (c)   degree of risk contained in
    (d)   anticipated weather for

Understanding Electrical Estimating | MikeHolt.com

4. As of 2022, there were over ____ electrical contractors in the United States competing for $225 billion worth of work, and competition is fierce.

    (a)   50,000
    (b)   75,000
    (c)   100,000
    (d)   150,000

1.3 What Is an Estimate?

5. Estimating is the process used to determine the ____ to complete a certain type and amount of work.

    (a)   time required
    (b)   cost
    (c)   permits required
    (d)   skills required

6. The purpose of estimating is to determine the cost of a project before you do the work. Estimating must at least consider the ____.

    (a)   cost of materials
    (b)   labor costs and availability
    (c)   overhead
    (d)   all of these

7. An accurate estimate is calculated by including indirect cost(s) for ____.

    (a)   labor
    (b)   material
    (c)   equipment and services
    (d)   all of these

8. An accurate estimate is calculated by including direct cost(s) for ____.

    (a)   material
    (b)   rental expense
    (c)   overhead and labor
    (d)   all of these

9. Indirect costs include ____.

   (a) employee benefits
   (b) business operational overhead
   (c) management expenses
   (d) all of these

10. ____ is added to the estimated total as the final step before submitting the bid.

    (a) Profit
    (b) Sales tax
    (c) Liability insurance
    (d) Payroll tax

1.4 Estimate Types

11. ____ must take into consideration variable job conditions, material costs, labor costs, labor availability, direct-job expenses, risks, and management costs (overhead).

    (a) Profitability
    (b) Time management
    (c) Estimating
    (d) Work-life balance

12. Estimates can be divided into ____ basic categories.

    (a) two
    (b) three
    (c) four
    (d) five

13. A basic type of estimate is ____ estimates.

    (a) preliminary
    (b) piece-rate
    (c) detailed
    (d) all of these

Understanding Electrical Estimating | MikeHolt.com

14. Preliminary estimates are generally based on ____.

    (a) the use of the facility
    (b) the square-foot dimensions
    (c) the type of construction
    (d) all of these

15. The preliminary or budget estimate provides the estimated cost along with a projected profit and overhead number during____.

    (a) the design phase
    (b) trades meetings
    (c) budget assessments
    (d) planning board meetings

16. Quantity or piece-rate estimates are common in several sectors of the electrical industry and are used for ____.

    (a) repetitive work
    (b) internal analysis
    (c) itemized work
    (d) any of these

17. The ____ estimate is the most accurate type of estimate.

    (a) limited scope
    (b) piece rate
    (c) detailed
    (d) budget

1.5 Estimates and Design Stages

18. Estimates are used to determine the cost of a project once the ____ has been established.

    (a) final drawing
    (b) approved plan
    (c) design
    (d) material list

19. The design drawings stage(s) is(are) the ____ drawings.

    (a) schematic
    (b) design development
    (c) construction
    (d) all of these

20. Schematic drawings are very general conceptual drawings and they contain ____.

    (a) a basic floorplan and elevations
    (b) window and door openings
    (c) ceiling and wall finishes
    (d) all of these

21. Design and development drawings are approximately ____ percent complete.

    (a) 25–30
    (b) 50–60
    (c) 75
    (d) 85

22. ____ drawings are the final stage of design drawings.

    (a) Schematic
    (b) Design
    (c) Construction
    (d) One-Line

23. Sometimes there are no drawings which mainly happens when an owner calls for ____.

    (a) minor alterations
    (b) maintenance
    (c) repairs
    (d) any of these

24. In cases where there are no drawings, you'll need to create the ____ and price it.

 (a) floor plans
 (b) design drawings
 (c) schematic drawings
 (d) scope of work

1.6 Estimating System

25. A good estimating system is a set of tools that help you quickly and accurately determine the ____ of a project that includes all anticipated costs.

 (a) profit
 (b) cost
 (c) sales tax
 (d) scheduling

26. Proper project management makes the difference between ____ for an accurately estimated project

 (a) profit and loss
 (b) winning and losing a bid
 (c) safe and hazardous working conditions
 (d) being slow and busy

27. The project budget is based on ____ and describes the material and labor required for each phase of the job and when the material and labor will be needed

 (a) the estimate
 (b) the personnel
 (c) delivery schedules
 (d) the bring-in-date

28. The largest risk on a project is ____.

 (a) weather
 (b) supply chain issues
 (c) labor cost
 (d) material costs

1.7 Estimating vs Bidding

29. Once you have the estimated project cost, you must calculate the _____ that will be presented to the owner or contractor.

    (a)   terms
    (b)   conditions
    (c)   selling price (bid price)
    (d)   anticipated delays

30. There are _____ basic bid types that are used to communicate the selling price of a job to the customer.

    (a)   two
    (b)   three
    (c)   four
    (d)   five

31. The basic bid type(s) that is(are) used to communicate the selling price of a job to the customer is(are) _____.

    (a)   Competitive
    (b)   Negotiated
    (c)   Best Value
    (d)   any of these

32. A _____ bid is a type of bid used to communicate the selling price of a job to the customer.

    (a)   competitive
    (b)   negotiated
    (c)   best value
    (d)   any of these

33. The _____ bid process requires competing contractors to submit bids, and the customer chooses from among them.

    (a)   competitive
    (b)   best value
    (c)   time and material
    (d)   negotiated

Understanding Electrical Estimating | MikeHolt.com

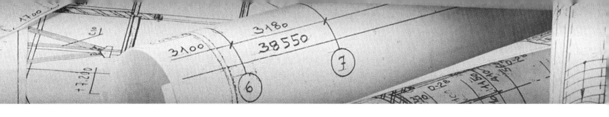

34. Negotiated bids are used when the electrical contractor works directly with the customer to negotiate a price based on the ____.

(a)   customer's needs
(b)   local zoning
(c)   fire subcodes
(d)   the insurance requirements

35. A ____ bid avoids competing to be the low bidder, but you need to know your cost, which means you need an estimate.

(a)   competitive
(b)   negotiated
(c)   best value
(d)   time and material

36. The ____ bid relies on alternate installation methods, gear packages, and fixture packages to be more cost-effective.

(a)   competitive
(b)   best value
(c)   time and material
(d)   negotiated

1.8 Can I Be Competitive?

37. Factors that impact a contractor's competitiveness can include ____.

(a)   management skills, experience
(b)   labor cost and productivity
(c)   other bidders
(d)   any of these

38. Many factors will determine if you can be competitive. The most significant factor is the condition of the market and the amount of ____.

(a)   labor available
(b)   available work
(c)   materials stocked
(d)   fuel costs

39. Most electrical contractors are concerned about their ability to ____, make money, and stay in business.

(a) be competitive
(b) be financially independent
(c) work from the home or office
(d) take time off

40. Other factors that affect a contractor's competitiveness include ____.

(a) wages
(b) cost of material (buying power)
(c) overhead
(d) any of these

41. When it comes to management skills, many electrical contractors are electricians without formal business management training; as a result, they don't do a very good job as ____.

(a) installers
(b) supervisors
(c) business owners
(d) salesmen

42. The more experience your company has with a given type of construction, the more able to do the job with less ____, resulting in a reduction in the estimated cost.

(a) material
(b) labor time
(c) aggravation
(d) paperwork

43. Risk must be considered when putting together an estimate for an unfamiliar type of work. The greater the perceived risk, the higher the ____ needs to be.

(a) material costs
(b) profit margin
(c) labor costs
(d) mark-ups

Understanding Electrical Estimating | MikeHolt.com

44. Make it a point to know your competition. Whenever possible it's important that you _____.

    (a) do not bid jobs with more than a few competitors
    (b) know your competition's capacity
    (c) monitor how busy your competitors are
    (d) all of these

45. Overhead costs represent between _____ of an electrical contractor's total sales.

    (a) between 10 and 20 percent
    (b) between 20 and 25 percent
    (c) between 20 and 40 percent
    (d) upwards of 50 percent

1.9 The Electrical Market

46. With _____, you can provide a quality installation at a fair price, which will be more cost-effective in the long run for your customers and better for your reputation.

    (a) a busy work schedule
    (b) proper management
    (c) a large number of employees
    (d) vast quantities of stock materials

47. New and expanding markets offer greater opportunities to develop new customers, possibly with _____ and greater profit margins

    (a) faster turnaround times
    (b) fewer competitors
    (c) incentives
    (d) company expansion

Notes...

Notes...

2nd Printing

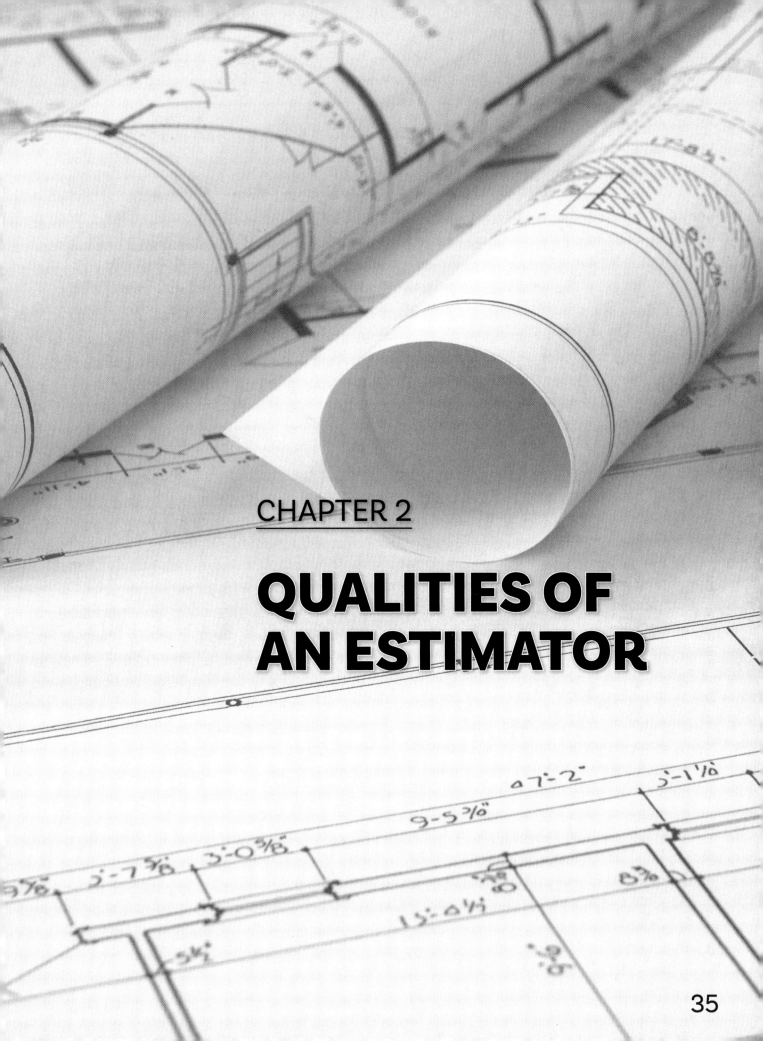

CHAPTER 2

QUALITIES OF
AN ESTIMATOR

2.1 Introduction

Now that you understand the important role that estimating plays in being profitable, you are ready to learn more about the person, the process, and what the final product should be. All of this can be understood clearly once you understand the responsibilities of an estimator and what resources are needed to meet those responsibilities. These qualities include:

2.2   Personal Qualities of an Estimator

2.3   Responsibilities of an Estimator

2.4   Field Experience and Job Skills

2.2 Personal Qualities of an Estimator

Some people are just built to be estimators. They find great satisfaction in balancing budgets and columns of numbers, or identifying small inconsistencies in projects after hours of scrutinizing.

A good estimator will have many of the qualities from the following list:

- Understands building construction
- Understands the *NEC* and local code requirements
- Visualizes the electrical installation
- Seeks out new products and installation methods
- Is skilled in technology
- Has a positive mental attitude
- Learns from mistakes
- Is careful, accurate, patient, and neat
- Is decisive and unintimidated by details
- Is fair and honest
- Is totally committed to get work done on time

2.3 Responsibilities of an Estimator

Now that you know the traits of a quality estimator, let's discuss some of his or her responsibilities, which include:

- Following the Rules
- Watching for Errors
- Managing Vendor Errors
- Placing Your Company First

Following the Rules

Plans and specifications work together to communicate the requirements needed for a complete project. The estimator must follow these guidelines to make sure that the work that is quoted complies.

This requires someone who is detail-oriented and not easily frustrated by long, tedious tasks. Thinking that "close enough is good enough," or that "you will get away without including a requirement" isn't a good strategy if you plan on staying in business. When an estimator lets this type of thinking creep into their work, it can bring a potentially profitable project to ruins before it even starts.

Watching for Errors

Another important function of the estimator is to review the bill of materials submitted with your vendor quotes to ensure they comply with the project requirements.

Something as simple as pricing the wrong brand of wire or raceway fitting can be a very costly mistake for the electrical contractor if it is not discovered before the bid is submitted.

Discuss any needed changes with the customer, contractor, and engineer, so that project documents can be updated before completing your estimate and submitting the price.

An estimator must be detail-oriented and have tremendous integrity. It's essential to look for errors and omissions in the plans and specifications during the early part of the estimating process.

If errors or omissions are found, the estimator must submit a request for information (RFI) for clarification to ensure the bid will meet the intent of the plans and the customer's needs. Counting on unnoticed omissions or design errors in the job documents to create a change order in your favor is a sure way to create conflict and lose money after the bid is awarded.

Ignoring errors in the plans and specifications shows a lack of concern for the customer, dishonesty, or lack of technical ability and professionalism. You are expected to be the expert and should guide your customer through the process.

Identifying problems early on will create rapport with the contractor and customer making it easier to discuss real changes in scope later in the project. An estimator must make sure the project can be built, and should compare the specifications to the *codes* in effect where the project is located.

Managing Vendor Errors

The quickest way to generate a bill of materials (BOM) to send a request for quote (RFQ) to your vendors is with estimating software. Most programs have a module designed to make this process very easy and accurate. Even when the list you submit is accurate, there is always a chance your vendor won't quote the right materials.

Make sure to review all bills of material (BOM) from each of your vendors to be sure they conform to the bid requirements before submitting them. A simple mistake can cost you a fortune.

If material is unavailable, discuss any changes with the customer and engineer so the project documents can be updated before completing your estimate and submitting the price.

Understanding Electrical Estimating | Mike Holt Enterprises

Placing Your Company First

The competitiveness of trying to win the job often drives us to do more than can be handled and can lead to cutting corners in our estimating methods—instead of putting the company first. While it's important to have the drive to win, here are a few estimating methods you must avoid at all costs:

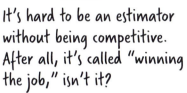

> It's hard to be an estimator without being competitive. After all, it's called "winning the job," isn't it?

- The Hero
- Shot-in-the-Dark
- Square-Foot King
- Guesstimator

The Hero

It's easy to think you must win the job. An estimate is based on your ability to do a specific type of work for a profit. Don't say, "If they can do it for that price, then so can I." You don't need to be a hero—you need to make money!

Since every company has different practices, employees, and skill sets, it's possible for your competitor to make a good profit on a job at a much lower price than you can.

If you weren't awarded the project, check your work for errors. Sometimes a simple error will take you out of the running. Other times, you can be glad that you weren't the one that made the mistake. In either case, make sure to learn from each project so you'll know what to look for the next time.

Shot-in-the-Dark

We often get busy and can't take the time to do an estimate correctly. The temptation is to take a shot in the dark. It would sound something like this..."Let's see, this project has five electrical drawing pages, so it should cost about $10,000. Yeah, that's the ticket, $2k per page..."

Understanding Electrical Estimating | MikeHolt.com

Chapter 2

Your price will be either very high or very low with a method like this, and ultimately you are playing with a ticking time bomb that will destroy your career and your business. An estimator must either do it right, or not do it at all.

The square-foot king and the guesstimator are examples of two "shot-in-the-dark" methods where the math just doesn't add up...

Square-Foot King

A common practice in some parts of the industry is to cost the job per square foot. Square foot pricing is often used by general contractors to put together budgets based on generic averages of the cost to build a particular type of building.

Unfortunately, because it represents the average job, it doesn't account for the many special considerations that make every project unique. Things like lighting packages, unusual wall construction types, or high ceilings can add a huge cost to the job and erase all hope of making money.

Although tracking square-foot costs can be a way to help you check your estimate, do not use this method to create an estimated cost.

Guesstimator

Another common method is to "look at the job" to decide what it's worth. This type of estimate is based on what someone remembers about a type of job, and how it feels based on past experiences.

These types of estimates usually result in a number that is "about a couple grand." While you can get lucky at times by guessing what it will cost, it's always better to stick with accurate estimating methods instead of "guesstimating" to make the most money on every job.

Understanding Electrical Estimating | Mike Holt Enterprises

40

2nd Printing

2.4 Field Experience and Job Skills

An estimate requires the individual to have the ability to mentally visualize the material items required, and the order in which they are installed to complete the job.

While it is possible to accurately estimate a job without electrical experience, it is unlikely for anything but the simplest of jobs. Even then, it will only be a matter of time before the lack of experience will cause an estimate to be terribly wrong.

Because electrical work is complex, the estimator needs to have electrical construction experience (preferably as an electrician) to envision the need for special equipment and/or services that will be required. Equipment such as scaffolding, man lifts, cranes, trenching, rigging services, and so on, must be included in the estimate in the proper quantity and duration.

The following are skills that every estimator must develop to be successful:

- Math Skills
- Negotiation Skills
- Communication Skills

Math Skills

Not only do you need to know what is required to complete the job, but you must be comfortable with numbers and basic math. During the course of the estimate and project, you will need to perform electrical, design, and budget calculations to determine the cost of a job, purchase materials, project profits, and cash flow needs.

While none of this is difficult, there is a lot of it, so make sure it's something you will enjoy.

Negotiation Skills

Since the estimator is usually most familiar with the job requirements, they are often expected to order the materials required to do the job, and set the delivery schedule.

It's important to have good negotiating skills with suppliers to get a competitive price. It's also important to have experience using alternate materials in case there is a problem obtaining timely delivery of any materials required.

Communication Skills

At some point the estimate information must be communicated to the project management team, so they know the budgets and bid requirements. A good estimator will be skilled at using the proper techniques to make this process efficient.

You may choose to use spreadsheets and e-mail to do this, but most estimating software can integrate with project management software to make the process seamless. If you choose this route, the estimator must take the time to enter the estimate data in detail and keep it current. This information will be essential for job costing once the project is complete.

Final Thoughts

You began this chapter with an understanding of *why* estimating is important, and you've completed this chapter with an understanding of what qualities an estimator should have.

The next step is to learn about the estimating process.

Use the information you learned in this chapter to answer the following questions.

Chapter 2—Review Questions

2.2 Personal Qualities of an Estimator

1. A good estimator will have qualities such as ____.

    (a) understands building construction
    (b) understands the NEC and local code requirements
    (c) visualizes the electrical installation
    (d) all of these

2.3 Responsibilities of an Estimator

2. Among the responsibilities of an estimator is to realize that plans and specifications work together, and to make sure that the work quoted ____.

    (a) is done quickly
    (b) is performed safely
    (c) complies
    (d) is easy to complete

3. Another important function of the estimator is to watch for errors and to review the ____ submitted with your vendor quotes to ensure they comply with the project requirements.

    (a) bill of materials
    (b) field reports
    (c) as built drawings
    (d) deliveries

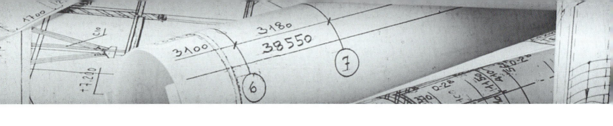

4. An estimator must be detail-oriented and have tremendous integrity. It's essential to look for errors and omissions in the plans and specifications during the _____ process

    (a) construction
    (b) early part of the estimating
    (c) plans examination
    (d) reconciliation

5. A common estimating practice in some parts of the industry is to cost the job per square foot. Square foot pricing is often used by _____ to put together budgets based on generic averages of the cost to build a particular type of building.

    (a) DIYers
    (b) general contractors
    (c) developers
    (d) city planners

2.4 Field Experience and Job Skills

6. Because electrical work is complex, the estimator needs to have electrical construction experience (preferably as a(an) _____).

    (a) electrician
    (b) apprentice electrician
    (c) journeyman electrician
    (d) master electrician

7. Good math skills are important during the course of the esti-mate and project, you will need to perform electrical, design, and budget calculations to _____, and cash flow needs...

    (a) determine the cost of a job
    (b) purchase materials
    (c) project profits
    (d) all of these

8. Since the estimator is usually most familiar with the job require-
    ments, they are often expected to order the materials required to
    do the job and ____.

    (a) distribute materials on site
    (b) inventory materials
    (c) set the delivery schedule
    (d) none of these

9. It's important that estimator's have good negotiating skills with
    suppliers to get ____.

    (a) timely deliveries
    (b) a competitive price
    (c) commissions from the supplier
    (d) substantial bonuses

Notes...

2nd Printing

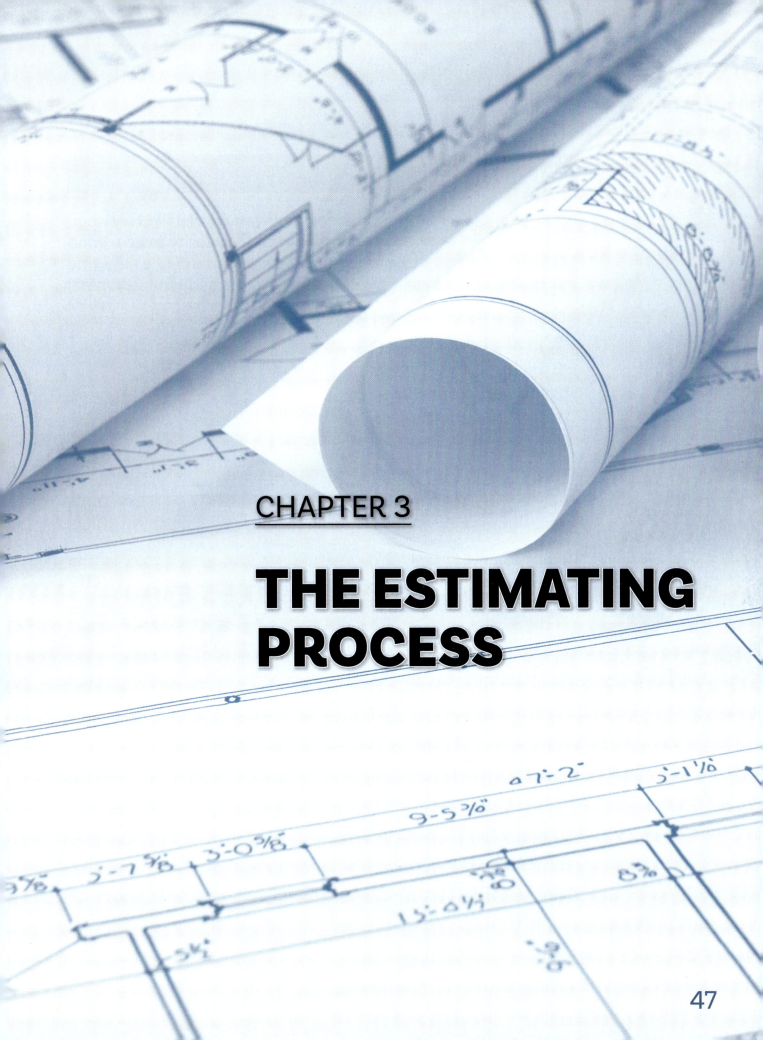

CHAPTER 3

THE ESTIMATING PROCESS

3.1 Introduction

An accurate estimate relies on accounting for every detail. Every workspace, tool, and method will contribute to your ability to do a good job, so it's important to give these details attention. Here are some things you must consider to ensure an accurate estimating process:

3.2   **The Estimating Workspace**

3.3   **The Estimating Tools**

3.4   **The Detailed Estimating Method**

3.5   **Estimate Accuracy**

3.6   **Estimating Techniques**

3.2 The Estimating Workspace

Before you even think of estimating a job, you need to have the proper workspace and tools. The workspace must be laid out efficiently and be located where the estimator will not be disturbed. It needs to be of adequate size, not just a closet with a desk.

Many business managers try to save money in this regard, only to lower the productivity of the estimators, and thereby raise the cost of doing business. The workspace should be designed to have comfortable lighting, and everything within reach of a seated position. Here are a couple of thoughts on furnishing your workspace.

Chair. Many estimators prefer to work with an adjustable-height swivel chair between two large tables or between a table and desk. A comfortable chair that rolls and has armrests will make a long day of takeoffs a lot more endurable, so do not try to save any money here. A properly fitting chair will pay for itself many times over.

Desk. A large desk with multiple horizontal surfaces is ideal to provide an adequate work area. A small work area will force you to continuously struggle to keep things organized and will waste valuable time.

Lighting. Make sure you have the right amount of light for your work area. Good overhead lighting that is dimmable is best when combined with well-placed task lighting.

Plan Racks. Plan racks neatly store drawings that are not in use. This keeps the work area organized, and your stress to a minimum.

Plan Table. If you must work with paper plans, purchase an inclined drafting table with enough space to lay the plans out flat. The table should have an edge on the bottom to keep the plans from sliding off. It should be able to be used from the desk chair without being raised or lowered.

Wall Space. A large clear wall in your work area is convenient for posting important information about the projects you are working on. Better yet, purchase a large screen TV that can display current documents and schedules.

Whiteboard. A whiteboard can be used for many functions such as scheduling, keeping track of jobs, and so forth. Even if you have a paperless office, a whiteboard is helpful for discussions, temporary notes, and other transient communication activities.

3.3 The Estimating Tools

We all know that performing a job without the proper tools often gives poor results, causes frustration, and takes longer than necessary. Proper estimating tools reduce human errors, increase efficiency, and quickly pay for themselves.

The estimator should have the following tools in proper condition:

Aspirin. You will need them. Seriously you will.

Computer. A good computer is a must in today's world. Most plans are in a digital format, and takeoff is commonly done on-screen using on-screen takeoff. This is not a negotiable purchase. If your machine goes down, you are out of commission. Look for a quiet machine that

Understanding Electrical Estimating | MikeHolt.com

does not give off a lot of heat. If you select a laptop for portability, make sure to pair it with a good docking station so you can connect additional equipment such as large monitors.

Software. Good estimating software will take some time to become comfortable with and master. The amount of time it takes to become adept at using a particular program depends on its complexity, and how much time you spend actually using it. The estimated cost for this type of software varies by type and purpose. See Chapter 9 on how to select estimating software.

Backup System. There are many options to back up your files to the cloud. Whether you choose Windows, iOS, or Linux as your operating system of choice, make sure you use a reliable cloud-based backup plan that you don't have to touch. It's the difference between losing thousands of hours of documentation and work, or a simple restore to a new machine.

Mouse and Keyboard. An estimator will be spending hours a day just sitting at their desk working. Don't be cheap. It's easy to cause repetitive stress injury to hands and wrists, so find the "perfect" keyboard and mouse. You may need to buy a few before you find the perfect one.

Monitors. Large high-resolution monitors are a great help when working on spreadsheets, digital plans, or project documentation. Two displays side by side allow several project documents to be open for reference simultaneously.

Drafting Tools. Make sure you have a set of architectural-scale rulers that are based on inches. While not essential, a set of engineering rulers will make quick measurements from paper civil or site drawings easier and more precise.

Digital Plan Wheel and Counter. A digital plan wheel is a scale ruler that can be rolled along the surface of paper drawings to measure circuit run lengths or room dimensions. You change the scale with the push of a button and is easy to read and use. Digital plan wheels also contain a counter feature and will usually connect to your computer to measure and count items on a plan via your estimating software.

Headphones. Noise-canceling headphones with music can help some people focus as they spend hours and hours estimating in an office environment.

Magnifying Glass. If you work with paper drawings, some details might be difficult to decipher without a magnifying glass. A pair of reading glasses might achieve the same effect hands-free.

Marking Tools. You will need colored pencils, pens, or fine- and large-tip highlighters to mark symbols on any drawing printouts, and to create as-built drawings for your team.

Printer/Scanner. In today's construction industry, project drawings and specifications are often being distributed electronically, but you may still need to download and print them. Purchase a multi-function copy/print/fax machine that is dedicated to the estimating space.

Most of your customers will prefer a paperless workflow, but you need to be able to accommodate those that do not. Consider a machine with a double sided ADF (automatic document feeder) and printing so both sides of multiple pages can be easily scanned or printed.

Use local or online printing services when possible for fast easy door-to-door delivery instead of purchasing a large printer or plotter.

Telephone. Phone numbers used by the estimating team should be dedicated numbers for use only by the estimating department. This will prevent tension with other office staff on bid day. If you must have a fax machine, utilize an e-fax service so your team can receive them as an e-mail instead of hassling with paper.

Understanding Electrical Estimating | MikeHolt.com

3.4 The Detailed Estimating Method

The correct method of estimating the cost of a job is the Detailed Method, and generally includes the following steps:

- Step 1: Understand the Project Scope
- Step 2: Complete the Takeoff
- Step 3: Create the Bill of Material
- Step 4: Determine the Cost of Labor and Materials
- Step 5: Extend and Total Material and Labor Costs
- Step 6: Estimate Summary
- Step 7: Overhead and Profit
- Step 8: Bid Analysis
- Step 9: Proposal

Step 1: Understand the Project Scope

The estimator must understand the scope of work to be completed according to the drawings and specifications. Read all the specifications and make notes of the items that affect the cost. Complete a checklist so you will know when the estimate is done. No guessing!

Step 2: Complete the Takeoff

Performing a takeoff is the process of counting and measuring to determine the material needed for the project. When you perform a takeoff, you are mentally visualizing the installation of the proposed electrical system. You are also counting and measuring the symbols on the drawings.

Use a systematic, repetitive system to reduce errors. If you have electrical trade experience related to the job, performing the takeoff is an easy step and actually very enjoyable—if estimating can be enjoyable.

Step 3: Create the Bill of Material

Information gathered from the Takeoff (Step 2) is used to create the bill of material (BOM)* required for the project.

This step can be very labor-intensive and is prone to errors unless you use estimating software.

*The bill of material (BOM) is discussed in more detail later.

Step 4: Determine the Cost of Labor and Materials

Once you have created the BOM (Step 3), it must be sent to your supplier(s) for pricing. You'll also need to calculate the job labor using the labor units* for each item.

This is also a very labor-intensive step and lends itself to errors if done by hand. Get comfortable using some type of computerized system to complete this step.

*Labor units are discussed in more detail later.

Step 5: Extend and Total Material and Labor Costs

Once you have the Cost of Labor and Materials (Step 4) for each item, it is time to determine the total material cost and labor. Extending means the price and labor unit of each item on the takeoff is multiplied by the takeoff quantity. Extending and totaling is simple but should be done by someone with good math skills with an eye for details.

This step is also very labor-intensive and prone to error if done by hand, so use a computer if possible. If you are using estimating software, this will be done automatically.

Understanding Electrical Estimating | MikeHolt.com

Step 6: Estimate Summary

Once the labor and material costs are totaled, they must be adjusted to reflect the job conditions. Incidental costs such as miscellaneous material, small tools, sales tax, subcontractor expenses, direct job costs, and so on, must also be added at this time. These costs should be included as line items in the estimate summary.

Step 7: Overhead and Profit

Most electrical contractors can do the takeoff and determine the cost of material and labor (especially if they use labor units), but applying the correct values for overhead, profit, and other final costs is where many fail. Understanding this step will determine your ability to make money.

Step 8: Bid Analysis

When the bid is complete, it must be verified to be sure no common estimating errors were made and ensure your price is valid.

Step 9: Proposal

When you have completed the bid, a written proposal must be submitted so there will not be any misunderstandings between you and your customer. The proposal must clearly state what your bid price includes and what it does not include.

3.5 Estimate Accuracy

There is no way to determine with 100 percent accuracy what a job is going to cost—no matter how great you are at estimating. As an estimator, you cannot control variables such as productivity, cost of material, or the activities of other trades.

Yet, all of these (and more) affect the bottom line. However, you can attempt to predict the cost of these variables within a reasonable level of certainty and accuracy.

What we must do is anticipate as much as we possibly can so a projected cost for the job can be determined. If we estimate correctly, and if everything we anticipate happens, we should complete the job reasonably close to our estimated cost.

Not all expenses can be anticipated, but experienced estimators accept a satisfactory margin of error in the accuracy of a bid. With increased experience and practice, you will also increase your speed in completing each estimate.

If you break the job down into its smallest possible parts, then the magnitude of any mistakes will be reduced and hopefully cancel each other out (the law of compensating errors). This also helps to keep the guesswork to a minimum.

No matter how great you are at estimating, there's no way to determine exactly what a job will cost. Changing jobsite variables will affect how much time and material it takes to complete the project. As with anything in life, the more experience you have, the more accurate and confident you will become in your bids.

Variables

Variables, such as employee productivity and the activities of other trades, will affect your bottom line. An estimator can predict the cost of these variables with a reasonable level of certainty using historical data coupled with their experience. The more historical data and experience an estimator has, the more accurate the estimate will be.

To reduce the impact of project variables on the estimate, break the project into its smallest possible parts when calculating costs. The law of compensating errors should take care of the rest.

> " The law of compensating errors shows us that because we almost always make multiple mistakes all at the same time, some to our favor and others to our detriment, the end result is that they cancel each other out.

Understanding Electrical Estimating | MikeHolt.com

Material

Material can be the most predictable part of the estimate (assuming that prices for copper and steel do not skyrocket), and if the pricing you used for the estimate was accurate in the first place.

Obviously, these prices are effective only during a certain time period and may be subject to change as material costs such as steel and copper fluctuate. During volatile pricing markets, it is very important that the bid includes a time window to address such cost variations. If you are estimating manually, errors in determining the bill of material, pricing, extending, and totaling can be significant.

A material budget must be given to the job supervisor to ensure the job is completed as estimated. In addition, don't overlook the impact of qualified project management to ensure the job is run according to the estimate.

Labor

Labor is more difficult to predict than material, but with job experience, labor can be calculated to within 10 percent for new work, and 20 percent for remodeling jobs. Keeping a file of completed jobs that are similar can assist in determining the labor adjustments needed in order to be competitive.

It's important to give a qualified project manager the estimate and labor budget to ensure the job is run according to plan. Have him or her send any needed adjustments to the estimator so that, if necessary, the labor units can be adjusted for the next job.

3.6 Estimating Techniques

There are a number of different methods to determine the estimated cost of a job that include:

2nd Printing

- Manual Estimating
- Computer-Assisted Estimating
- Estimating Service

Manual Estimating

Manual estimates are good for very small projects and have been used by electrical contractors for over a hundred years. This technique is great if you are a one-man show and have control of every aspect of the process yourself. If you have employees working across multiple jobsites, manual estimates have a number of disadvantages.

Disadvantages

While manual estimates do have a few advantages, they also have a few very distinct disadvantages which include:

- Time
- Cost
- Bid Inaccuracy
- Bill of Material Errors
- Lack of Project Management
- Response to Changes

Time. It takes a lot of time to estimate a job manually. A busy contractor will typically produce a bottom-line price and not much more. Estimates are likely to become backlogged because they are so time consuming.

Today, more than any other time in history, we operate in an age of instant information and expected response. Because of cell phones, e-mail, and the internet, customers demand—and expect—to receive information almost instantaneously. Few customers are willing to give you the time you need to prepare an accurate manual bid.

Cost. A manual estimate has the highest labor cost per estimate since it takes so much time. Every hour that is spent completing an estimate costs the company labor money that could be used for management or job installation.

As a result, using a computer-based estimate to increase efficiency will typically make better financial sense. Let's assume you are a small contractor, and you win one job out of every four bids you submit.

If you successfully win one job out of every four bids you submit (25%), and you spend an average of 4 hours to estimate each job at $50 per hour (including benefits). It will cost you $800 for every job that you win [4 hrs × 4 jobs = 16 hrs × $50].

If you are able to reduce the amount of time spent on each bid, then the overhead cost per bid will also decrease, and that is where the computer estimating software shines.

 Cost Example: Formula: Overhead = Qty of Jobs Bid x Hours to Bid x Estimator Wage

Overhead = 4 jobs x 4 hrs x $50/hr
Overhead = 16 x 50
Overhead = $800

Note: If you only win one of the jobs, it will cost $800 to win the job.

Bid Inaccuracy. The pressure of completing the estimate quickly to move on to the next estimate can result in increased errors.

Bill of Material Errors. It's difficult to accurately create and price the BOM manually.

Lack of Project Management. Without estimating software, smaller electrical contractors don't typically manage their jobs efficiently. It's too labor intensive. Because of the time it takes to manually extract project management information without the use of estimating software, most electrical contractors just do not do it if they estimate a job manually. The result is that the job cannot be tracked to ensure it is properly managed.

Response to Changes. It is very difficult to cope with last-minute changes to the drawings or specifications if you have to recalculate a manual estimate.

Sometimes the change is so great that you do not have enough time to estimate the job in a timely manner. This can result in an attempt to make an educated guess, or you may just give up and not submit a bid at all. Either way, this is *not* a good business practice.

Computer-Assisted Estimating

Computer-assisted estimating (use of software) is similar to manual estimating, except the computer forces you to be consistent and the math calculations are completed automatically. Computer-assisted estimating is only as good as the person using the system, so be sure you're adequately trained to use your software.

The many advantages of using estimating software include:

Bill of Material. Software can automatically generate a BOM for suppliers and project management.

Increased Bid Accuracy. With estimating software, errors with pricing material and the application of labor units will be significantly reduced, as compared to the manual method. There are no transpositions of numbers, no mistakes on the totals, and no errors when transferring numbers to the estimate summary. Your bids will be clearer, more legible, and more professional in appearance.

Understanding Electrical Estimating | MikeHolt.com

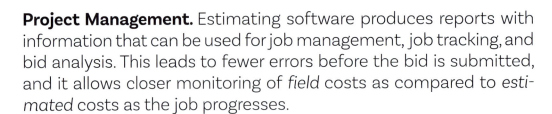

Project Management. Estimating software produces reports with information that can be used for job management, job tracking, and bid analysis. This leads to fewer errors before the bid is submitted, and it allows closer monitoring of *field* costs as compared to *estimated* costs as the job progresses.

Reduced Overhead. The cost of producing an estimate is much lower than the manual method.

Response to Changes. It's much easier to accommodate last-minute changes to drawings or specifications if you can tweak a quantity and the software recalculates all the totals for you. This avoids you having to manually recalculate the bid to accommodate changes to the project scope. You won't feel as much pressure to rush an estimate when there are last-minute fixture quotes, switchgear quotes, or changes that must be accounted for.

Time. Estimating software is at least four times more efficient than the manual technique. What takes eight hours manually, can take less than two hours with estimating software. Not only that, but this also increases the odds of winning a job.

Estimating Service

An estimating service is an agency that you pay to produce an estimate. You then review their estimate, make any needed adjustments, and prepare a bid. When an estimating service produces an estimate, you need to review the information to ensure that the estimate is accurate, matches your styles of installation, and is complete.

You might use an estimating service to double-check an estimate you have completed, or when you do not have the time to do it yourself. An estimating service is an excellent tool to help you gain estimating experience while reducing risk.

Cost. With an estimating service, you will know in advance what it costs to estimate a job. Their fees are generally based on the total electrical bid dollar amount and are provided to you prior to them performing the estimate.

This will allow you to consider if the job opportunity is worth spending your hard-earned money to estimate.

Final Thoughts

You began this chapter with a good understanding of the estimating process from Chapter 1 and a list of all the important qualities of a good estimator from Chapter 2. In this chapter you have been introduced to the key concepts of the estimating process, and what some of the advantages and disadvantages of the different estimating systems are.

Armed with a solid foundation, let's move on to Chapter 4 and learn what a takeoff is, and how to accurately complete this major step in the estimating process.

Understanding Electrical Estimating | MikeHolt.com

Use the information you learned in this chapter to answer the following questions.

Chapter 3—Review Questions

3.1 Introduction

1. An accurate estimate relies on ____ for every detail.

   (a) accounting
   (b) price lists
   (c) books
   (d) product samples

3.2 The Estimating Workspace

2. Before you even think of estimating a job, you need to have the proper ____ and tools.

   (a) price lists
   (b) books
   (c) workspace
   (d) attitude

3. Considerations for furnishing your workspace should include ____.

   (a) a properly fitted chair
   (b) a large enough desk
   (c) an inclined drafting table
   (d) all of these

3.3 The Estimating Tools

4. Trying to perform a job without the proper tools often gives poor results. The estimator should have ____.

    (a)   a good computer
    (b)   good estimating software
    (c)   a file backup system
    (d)   all of these

5. Large high-resolution monitors are a great help when working on spreadsheets, digital plans, or ____.

    (a)   meeting notes
    (b)   project documentation
    (c)   email
    (d)   codes materials

3.4 The Detailed Estimating Method

6. The correct method of estimating the cost of a job is the ____.

    (a)   Detailed Method
    (b)   Square-Foot Method
    (c)   Comparison Method
    (d)   Artificial Intelligence (AI) Method

7. In understanding the scope of a project, the estimator must understand the work to be completed according to ____.

    (a)   the drawings and specifications
    (b)   personal experience
    (c)   the labor costs involved
    (d)   the material delivery schedule

8. The second step in the detailed estimate process is to complete the ____.

    (a)   project document filing system
    (b)   introductions of all parties to the project
    (c)   takeoff
    (d)   obtain plans approvals

Understanding Electrical Estimating | MikeHolt.com

9. A ____ is the process of counting and measuring to determine the material needed for the project.

    (a) plans review
    (b) takeoff
    (c) plans evaluation
    (d) Scoping

10. Information gathered from the takeoff is used to create the ____ required for the project.

    (a) initial order
    (b) material delivery schedule
    (c) anticipated completion date
    (d) bill of material (BOM)

11. Once you have created the bill of material (BOM), it must be sent to your supplier(s) for ____.

    (a) pricing
    (b) review
    (c) discounting
    (d) product substitutions

12. Determining the labor units is a very labor-intensive step and lends itself to errors if ____.

    (a) left to others
    (b) done by hand
    (c) determined by your supplier(s)
    (d) left to memory

13. When completing the estimate summary after the labor and material costs are totaled, they must be adjusted to reflect ____.

    (a) job conditions
    (b) incidental costs
    (c) subcontractor expenses
    (d) all of these

14. The final step in the detailed estimate process is to ____.

    (a)   apply overhead and profit
    (b)   perform a bid analysis
    (c)   submit the proposal
    (d)   apply your license seal

3.5 Estimate Accuracy

15. The only way to determine with 100 percent accuracy what a job might cost is ____.

    (a)   use artificial intelligence (AI)
    (b)   use estimating software
    (c)   seek advice from more experienced estimators
    (d)   100 percent accuracy is not possible

16. Estimate accuracy is affected by variables such as ____.

    (a)   productivity
    (b)   cost of materials
    (c)   activities of other trades
    (d)   all of these

17. Variables, such as employee productivity and the activities of other trades, will affect your bottom line. An estimator can predict the cost of these variables with a reasonable level of certainty using ____ and their experience.

    (a)   historical data
    (b)   updated plans
    (c)   staff meetings
    (d)   artificial intelligence

18. In order to promote estimate accuracy, a material budget must be given to the ____ to ensure the job is completed as estimated.

    (a)   job supervisor
    (b)   construction supervisor
    (c)   customer
    (d)   general contractor

Understanding Electrical Estimating | MikeHolt.com

19. When considering estimate accuracy, labor is more difficult to predict than material, but with job experience, labor can be calculated to within ____ percent for new work, and ____ percent for remodeling jobs

    (a) 2, 5
    (b) 5, 10
    (c) 10, 15
    (d) 10, 20

3.6 Estimating Techniques

20. There are a number of techniques to determine the estimated cost of a job which can include ____.

    (a) a manual estimate
    (b) a computer assisted estimate
    (c) an estimating service
    (d) all of these

21. Manual estimates are good for ____ and have been used by electrical contractors for over a hundred years.

    (a) small profit
    (b) efficiency
    (c) very small projects
    (d) clarity

22. A disadvantage of the manual estimating technique is that it takes a lot of ____ to estimate a job manually.

    (a) time
    (b) experience
    (c) resources
    (d) space

23. The computer-assisted estimating technique (use of software) is similar to manual estimating, except the computer forces you to be ____.

    (a) consistent
    (b) focused
    (c) thorough
    (d) alert

24. Increased bid accuracy is one advantage of using estimating software as errors with pricing material and the application of labor units will be ____.

    (a) non-existent
    (b) tolerable
    (c) significantly reduced
    (d) more profitable

25. An estimating service is an agency that you pay to produce an estimate. When an estimating service produces an estimate, you need to review the information to ensure that the estimate is accurate, matches your styles of installation, and ____.

    (a) is reasonable
    (b) is complete
    (c) is available in a digital format
    (d) includes a written proposal

Understanding Electrical Estimating | MikeHolt.com

Notes...

2nd Printing

CHAPTER 4

THE TAKEOFF

4.1 Introduction

Estimating is both a science and an art form. Part of the science of estimating is to accurately determine how many of each part and each task must be performed so that you can calculate an accurate labor and material budget. This process is called the takeoff and involves physically counting each item on a bid and recording this count on a worksheet.

A good takeoff is based on all project documents, not just the plans, so it's important to complete the takeoff in an orderly fashion that can be repeated. This allows you to consistently produce quality information that can be used to estimate the cost to complete your scope of work without missing anything. A quality takeoff will consider the following:

4.2   **The Takeoff Sequence**

4.3   **The Takeoff**

4.4   **Takeoff Systems**

4.5   **Determining the Bill of Material**

4.6   **Determining Labor**

4.7   **Pricing Material and Labor**

4.8   **Extension**

4.9   **Historical Data**

4.2 The Takeoff Sequence

To takeoff a job, there is a sequence of steps you must complete before you can do the next. If any step is completed incorrectly (or skipped), the subsequent steps will be wrong. If you hurry one step to get to the next, the results will be unreliable, and you will have wasted all your estimating time. Here is the list of things to review for an accurate takeoff:

- Understand the Scope
- Obtain Project Documents
- Organize Project Documents
- Request for Information
- Using Different Types of Worksheets

Understand the Scope

Once you have determined a job is a good fit for your company and decide to submit a bid, learn everything you can about the scope of the work by reviewing the complete set of drawings and specifications. The scope of work describes the work that needs to be done for a project.

Make sure to at least look over the other trade drawings to make sure that there aren't details missing from the electrical drawings. As computer-aided design has become the standard method to draw plans, a little mistake on the part of a draftsman can omit important details from the electrical plans that may impact your final price.

Obtain Project Documents

Your first step in preparing for a takeoff is to make sure to obtain a complete set of project documents. Each document contains information that will help you interpret the intention of the drawings, and the owner's needs. Make sure to do your due diligence on the front side so you don't have to stop in the middle of the estimate to chase after documents. Documents that you need to complete your estimate include:

- Site Plan
- Architectural Plan
- Floor Plans
- Request for Information
- Specifications
- Jobsite Visit

Understanding Electrical Estimating | MikeHolt.com

Site Plan

The Site Plan is typically identified by the letter "C" (Civil) preceding the page numbers. These drawings show the civil engineering portion of the project, indicate how the building is situated on real property, and any existing or future site improvements. This is also where the parking lot lights, landscape lights, and utility connections are shown.

Use the site plan to determine any dimensions for estimating site work.

Architectural Plan

The architectural plan is typically identified by the letter "A" (Architectural) preceding the page numbers. These architectural drawings will include information such as building and structural materials, wall cross-sections and dimensions, wall and floor finishes, and building elevations.

These plans are helpful as they show any special construction of finishes and high-reach locations. This information will assist in determining if any additional special labor and/or equipment might be needed to install your equipment and fixtures.

Floor Plans

The floor plans are specific to each of the trades and contain specific installation information about the different systems on a project. The floor plans are typically identified by the letter "M" (Mechanical), "P" (Plumbing), and "E" (Electrical), and the pages are numbered as M-1, P-1, and E-1 etc. Floor plans are trade-specific, but the plumbing and mechanical plans often contain information for the electrical contractor that is not apparent on the electrical floor plan.

The electrical plans will often consist of multiple pages containing lighting layouts, power layouts, panel schedules, additional specifications, symbol legends, and circuit diagrams, so make sure you review them all.

Understanding Electrical Estimating | Mike Holt Enterprises

Request for Information

If there is any ambiguity or uncertainty on what is shown on the drawings, submit an RFI (Request for Information) to the person in charge of the project. Make sure you always communicate everything in writing when it comes to drawings. A verbal conversation can be forgotten or misunderstood and can lead to big problems later.

Specifications

Some jobs will have written specifications that are additional requirements governing the material to be used and the work to be performed on the project. Specifications are designed to simplify the task of interpreting the drawings, and to make sure all bidders are providing the same product for the bid price.

Product brand, conductor, and wiring method types are commonly found in the specifications. Items such as earthwork may be covered in parts of the specifications that seem unrelated to your scope of work, so be sure to review all sections of items that could impact your price. Specifications are a part of the contract bidding documents and must be considered in your bids.

> Poor drawings and specifications often result in confusion and an increase in the time it takes to complete the estimate and the job. Make sure your contract is clear as to what revision of the plans and specifications your price reflects and any RFI responses that were considered as part of the price.

Construction project specifications are typically organized by divisions defined by the Construction Specification Institute (CSI).

The current system for construction specifications has 48 divisions. There are five divisions that are specific to the electrical trade:

Specification Divisions (CSI)	
Division 25	Integrated Automation
Division 26	Electrical
Division 27	Communications
Division 28	Electronic Safety & Security
Division 48	Electrical Power Generation

Understanding Electrical Estimating | MikeHolt.com

Jobsite Visit

Whenever it's possible, visit the jobsite before you bid on the job.

Document jobsite conditions or special considerations using your phone, tablet, or a digital camera. This way you don't forget important details and can answer your own questions as you complete the estimate. This is especially important when doing remodel work as the pictures will remind you of details you may have forgotten.

Finally, be sure to take notes of anything important you discover during your site visit. Items such as existing colors or device brands can have a significant impact on your final price..

Organize Project Documents

To estimate a job quickly and accurately, use proper estimating forms and worksheets to organize the information you have collected from the project documents. These forms and worksheets will save time, create consistency, and help reduce errors. They also help serve as a reminder of items that are easily omitted or forgotten.

Estimating software usually contains customizable preset forms for printing and/or e-mailing your proposals. You can also use a computer to design custom worksheets or order customized forms from various vendors online.

Some things that will help you stay organized include the following:

- Job Folder
- Use a Scanner
- Estimate Record Worksheet
- Review the Plans
- Review the Specifications
- Create the Specifications Checklist

Job Folder

Create a job folder to keep your bid notes, job information sheet, takeoff worksheets, bill of material worksheets, quote sheets, summary sheet, and other papers associated with the estimate. You should do this for the traditional paper records, and also create a matching electronic one on your computer.

If you find yourself doing a large volume of estimates, it's critical to leverage software to streamline the process. There are numerous software packages available that allow you to keep all your information in one place from start to finish.

During the estimating process, you will manage large amounts of information. You must be organized to account for all the requirements in your estimated cost.

Use a Scanner

Scan all paper documents to your computer so you don't have to manage paper. You can use your phone camera and a scanning app if it's only a few papers.

Estimate Record Worksheet

Use an Estimate Record Worksheet to organize job details. This form contains pertinent job information, such as job name, job location/address, telephone numbers, owner's name, general contractor, architect, engineer, and to whom the bid is to be submitted.

This worksheet can be kept on paper, on a spreadsheet, or in estimating software. Once you have completed the estimate record worksheet, keep it handy for future reference.

For example, hang a paper copy of the estimate record worksheet up on the wall, or create a desktop shortcut for an electronic one. This information will be useful when working on your estimate and creating a bid proposal.

Understanding Electrical Estimating | MikeHolt.com

Estimate Record Worksheet

Estimate Job Number:	Date:	
Contractor:	Contact	
Address:	City:	State:
Office Phone:	Cell Phone:	
E-mail:	Other:	
Owner:	Contact:	
Address:	City:	State:
Office Phone:	Cell Phone:	
E-mail:	Other:	
Job Name:	Bid Due Date:	
Job Address:	City:	State
Plans and Specifications:		
Date of Plans:	Number of Drawing Pages:	
Architect:	Phone:	E-mail:
Engineer:	Phone:	E-mail:
Telephone:	Phone:	E-mail:
Electric:	Phone:	E-mail:
Electrical Inspector:	Phone:	E-mail:

Estimate Record Worksheet (continued)
Other:
Other:
Other:
Notes:

Review the Plans

Before counting items on the plan, review all plan pages and identify easily overlooked items. Underline, circle, or highlight important and/or unusual items that can affect the estimate.

Plans are often crowded with details that are difficult to identify but important to the final price. This is one area in which on-screen takeoff software excels. Make sure to make multiple passes over the drawings so you catch the little details that you may miss on the first review.

Take a close look at all drawing legends, details, notations, and symbols. If you see something in the legend that's not on the drawing, take care to ensure you didn't overlook anything.

Some projects will have device and fixture counts available with the bid documents. These are a great way to double check your work, and make sure you didn't miss anything.

Watch for control wiring, underground wiring, area lighting, signs, and outdoor equipment that may not be a normal part of the job.

Become familiar with the entire installation and check for any special or unusual features such as elevated ceilings. Check to see if proper working space is provided for the electrical equipment, the locations of utilities, and so on.

Understanding Electrical Estimating | MikeHolt.com

Case Study No. 1: A friend of mine, who was just getting started in business, did not read the note on the drawing that required him to replace 180 ft of 4/0 AWG service conductors with 500 kcmil service conductors.

The Result: He underbid the job by $4,000 on a $35,000 job and won the job losing $4,000!

 Case Study No. 2: The drawings indicated that the electrical contractor was required to install three of the owner's fixtures. The contractor didn't have sufficient information on the fixtures and figured 3 hours for each fixture during the bid. The actual fixtures weighed over 500 lb. each and required three men three days to install them!

The Result: He won the bid and lost 15 hours of labor.

 Case Study No. 3: During the estimating takeoff process, a symbol for a lighting fixture was overlooked by the electrical contractor. The owner was providing the fixtures, but the wiring and labor costs for the installation were $125 each.

The Result: There were 40 of these fixtures indicated on the plans throughout the building, so the contractor lost $5,000!

You may be able to work some of these details out after you're on the job, but always assume you're going to pay if you miss them.

Review the Specifications
Now that you have reviewed the plans, it's time to begin reviewing the specification documents to understand the details of the job.

Carefully read the specifications documents and all notes on the drawings so that you have a clear understanding of the scope of the project and the bid requirements before you begin the actual takeoff.

Make notes on the drawings of important details (like alternate options and allowances) you must remember while completing the estimate. Identify any alternate options for material or installation methods and allowances to be included in the bid. Make sure to watch for specific brand or vendor requirements, so that you provide a bid that meets the specifications.

> **Word of Caution:** If you are required to use specific subcontractors, provide a bond, or use a specific brand, make sure you can comply before you do all the work to submit a bid that you don't qualify to perform.

If the owner is supplying material, such as a fixture package, remember to deduct only the material cost of the item(s) supplied *not* the labor, profit, or overhead. You will still incur the same costs of handling, storing, installation, labor for any warranty, and all the other overhead costs and risk factors associated with that material.

Underline, circle, or highlight important and/or unusual items that can affect the estimate. Some estimators will circle these items before doing the takeoff, and only highlight them after taking care of the item in the estimate.

Determine who is responsible for painting exposed conduits, trenching, backfill, concrete work, patching, cleanup, temporary power, and so on. Find out if the use of special equipment or overtime is required.

Don't take anything for granted. You may be able to work some of these details out after you're on the job with other sub-contractors, but always assume you're going to pay to have them done when determining your cost.

Understanding Electrical Estimating | MikeHolt.com

Case Study No. 4: According to the specifications, a contractor was required to provide a video projector. He priced a similar brand and model that cost $5,000 because he didn't make the time to price out the exact model specified.

The Result: The owner required the exact model specified in the plans—not the proposed alternate. The specified model cost $18,000 not $5,000 resulting in a $13,000 loss!

Create the Specifications Checklist

To help you keep track of the drawings and specifications details, complete the specifications checklist worksheet as you proceed through the estimate. You will need this information at different stages of the process. Make pertinent notes, such as scope and wiring methods for reference as you complete the various steps of the estimate.

Use the list below to create a checklist of important items to be checked off when the estimate is near completion. This list is best kept on a spreadsheet or paper separate from the bid so that you can check it off as you go through the bid documents.

Specifications Checklist		
Labor-Unit Adjustment		
1.	Building Conditions	
2.	Change Orders	
3.	Concealed and Exposed Wiring	
4.	Construction Schedule	
5.	Job Factors	
6.	Labor Skill (Efficiency)	
7.	Ladder and Scaffold	
8.	Management	
9.	Material	

Specifications Checklist (continued)

10.	Off Hours and Occupied	
11.	Overtime	
12.	Remodel (Old Work)	
13.	Repetitive Factor	
14.	Restrictive Working Conditions	
15.	Shift Work	
16.	Teamwork	
17.	Temperature	
18.	Weather and Humidity	
Labor Adjustment		
Additional Labor		
1.	As-Built Plans	
2.	Demolition	
3.	Energized Parts	
4.	Environmental Hazards	
5.	Excavation, Trenching, and Backfill	
6.	Fire Seals	
7.	Job Location	
8.	Match-Up of Existing Equipment	
9.	Miscellaneous Material Items	
10.	Mobilization (Start-up)	
11.	Nonproductive Labor	
12.	OSHA Compliance	
13.	Plans and Specifications	
14.	Public Safety	
15.	Security	
16.	Shop Time	
17.	Site Conditions	
18.	Subcontract Supervision	
19.	Temporary and/or Standby Power	
Hour Adder		

Understanding Electrical Estimating | MikeHolt.com

Specifications Checklist (continued)	
Direct-Job Expenses	
1. As-Built Plans	$
2. Business and Occupational Fees	$
3. Engineering Drawings	$
4. Equipment Rental	$
5. Field Office Expenses	$
6. Fire Seals	$
7. Warranty	$
8. Insurance—Special	$
9. Miscellaneous	$
10. Mobilization	$
11. OSHA Compliance	$
12. Out-of-Town Expenses	$
13. Parking Fees	$
14. Permits/Inspection Fees	$
15. Public Safety	$
16. Recycle Fees	$
17. Storage and Handling	$
18. Subcontract: _____	$
19. Supervision Cost	$
20. Temporary Wiring:	$
21. Lighting	$
22. Power	$
23. Maintenance	$
24. Testing	$
25. Trash	$
26. Utility Cost	$
Total Direct Cost	$

82

Specifications Checklist (continued)

Other Final Costs

1.	Allowances/Contingency	$
2.	Back-Charges	$
3.	Bond	$
4.	Completion Penalty	$
5.	Finance Cost	$
6.	Gross Receipts or Net Profit Tax	$
7.	Inspection Problems	$
8.	Retainage	$
Total Other Cost		$

Other Considerations

1.	Conductor Size—Minimum?	
2.	Raceway Size—Minimum?	
3.	Control Wiring Responsibility?	
4.	Concrete Cutting and/or Core Boring Responsibility?	
5.	Demolition Responsibility?	
6.	Excavation/Backfill Responsibility?	
7.	Painting Responsibility?	
8.	Patching Responsibility?	
9.	Special Equipment?	
10.	Specification Grade Devices or Fittings?	

Request for Information

If you don't understand something in the drawings or specifications, you might have the tendency to delay the estimate until the last minute. This will result in a late bid, or worse yet, bidding the job at the last minute without the correct information.

Understanding Electrical Estimating | MikeHolt.com

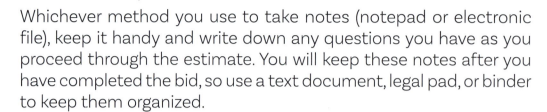

Whichever method you use to take notes (notepad or electronic file), keep it handy and write down any questions you have as you proceed through the estimate. You will keep these notes after you have completed the bid, so use a text document, legal pad, or binder to keep them organized.

If there is anything that is unclear, get the answer as soon as possible—don't wait until the last minute. Submit a Request For Information (RFI) to the architect or engineer, if necessary, but do it immediately. An RFI often requires days to be processed so that a formal response can be provided.

> **Word of Caution:** Never submit a bid based on verbal answers to questions.

Always capture conversations in a follow-up e-mail or other written response. If you're keeping paper job records, make sure to print out the responses to these questions and add them to your file

Keep a request for information (RFI) log in your job folder and include this with your proposal.

Using e-mail instead of the phone can save a lot of time and will create an electronic documentation trail. If you use text messages or the phone, make sure you write down the answer to your question on the notepad (or the electronic file) when you receive it.

Follow up a phone call or text message with an e-mail noting key details, "Per our conversation today, the following will be included in my proposal."

If you don't receive satisfactory answers to your questions, then either list the exclusions in your proposal, or withdraw your request to bid the job at all. It's better to not bid a job at all, than to be left in a difficult situation where you may lose time, money, or ruin a relationship with a vendor or contractor.

Using Different Types of Worksheets

Different types of construction, such as residential, commercial, or industrial, lend themselves to different types of estimating forms or worksheets. In addition, different types of forms and worksheets are required for different parts of the estimate.

Estimating software usually contains customizable preset forms for printing and/or e-mailing your proposals. You can also use a computer to design custom worksheets or order customized forms from various vendors online.

4.3 The Takeoff

Once you have all your documents and information organized it's time to start counting! The takeoff is the action of counting symbols and measuring lengths that can be used to determine the amount of labor and bill of material needed to complete the job. A proper takeoff provides all the numbers needed to complete the estimate so that there is little need to refer to the drawings or specifications. You can manually takeoff a project or use a computer-based system. In either case, the basic steps are the same.

Manual

When you do a manual takeoff on paper or digital plans, follow a specific color code to identify those items taken off.

Be sure to note what color you use for each step so you won't forget, or so someone else can pick up where you left off if necessary. Be consistent between bids to create a system that allows fast reference later if needed.

The following table contains a sample of a sequence and color code to use to identify those items taken off.

Understanding Electrical Estimating | MikeHolt.com

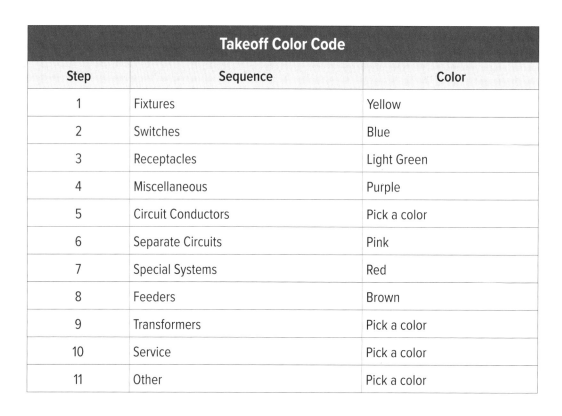

Takeoff Color Code		
Step	Sequence	Color
1	Fixtures	Yellow
2	Switches	Blue
3	Receptacles	Light Green
4	Miscellaneous	Purple
5	Circuit Conductors	Pick a color
6	Separate Circuits	Pink
7	Special Systems	Red
8	Feeders	Brown
9	Transformers	Pick a color
10	Service	Pick a color
11	Other	Pick a color

Color Identification

When you have finished the takeoff, your drawings should be a colored representation of the electrical work that needs to be installed. **Figure 4-1**

Some people prefer to simply place a check mark on the items they have taken off. **Figure 4-2**

If you didn't receive a full set of drawings that you can mark up, then you need to make a full-size copy, which can be done at most copy centers. Attempting to estimate a job without color coding the drawings will lead to mistakes and errors.

Computer Takeoff

If you are using software to do an on-screen takeoff, make sure to use the same colors and system used for a paper takeoff. This will make it easier to cross over between the two systems if part of the bid ends up in your estimating software, and part of it is on paper.

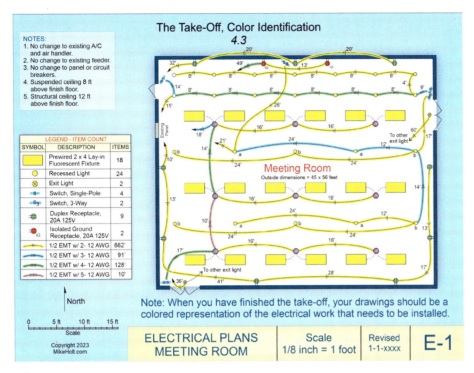

Figure 4–1

The Take-Off, Color Identification
4.3

NOTES:
1. No change to existing A/C and air handler.
2. No change to existing feeder.
3. No change to panel or circuit breakers.
4. Suspended ceiling 8 ft above finish floor.
5. Structural ceiling 12 ft above finish floor.

LEGEND - ITEM COUNT		
SYMBOL	DESCRIPTION	ITEMS
	Prewired 2 x 4 Lay-in Fluorescent Fixture	18
	Recessed Light	24
	Exit Light	2
	Switch, Single-Pole	4
	Switch, 3-Way	2
	Duplex Receptacle, 20A 125V	9
	Isolated Ground Receptacle, 20A 125V	2
	1/2 EMT w/ 2- 12 AWG	662'
	1/2 EMT w/ 3- 12 AWG	91'
	1/2 EMT w/ 4- 12 AWG	128'
	1/2 EMT w/ 5- 12 AWG	10'

North

Scale: 0 5 ft 10 ft 15 ft

Copyright 2023 MikeHolt.com

Meeting Room
Outside dimensions = 45 x 56 feet

Note: When you have finished the take-off, your drawings should be a colored representation of the electrical work that needs to be installed.

| ELECTRICAL PLANS MEETING ROOM | Scale 1/8 inch = 1 foot | Revised 1-1-xxxx | E-1 |

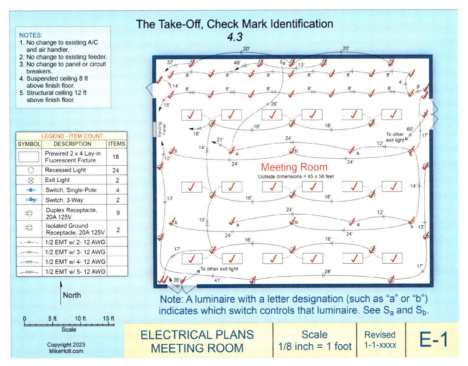

Figure 4–2

The Take-Off, Check Mark Identification
4.3

NOTES:
1. No change to existing A/C and air handler.
2. No change to existing feeder.
3. No change to panel or circuit breakers.
4. Suspended ceiling 8 ft above finish floor.
5. Structural ceiling 12 ft above finish floor.

LEGEND - ITEM COUNT		
SYMBOL	DESCRIPTION	ITEMS
	Prewired 2 x 4 Lay-in Fluorescent Fixture	18
	Recessed Light	24
	Exit Light	2
	Switch, Single-Pole	4
	Switch, 3-Way	2
	Duplex Receptacle, 20A 125V	9
	Isolated Ground Receptacle, 20A 125V	2
	1/2 EMT w/ 2- 12 AWG	
	1/2 EMT w/ 3- 12 AWG	
	1/2 EMT w/ 4- 12 AWG	
	1/2 EMT w/ 5- 12 AWG	

North

Scale: 0 5 ft 10 ft 15 ft

Copyright 2023 MikeHolt.com

Meeting Room
Outside dimensions = 45 x 56 feet

Note: A luminaire with a letter designation (such as "a" or "b") indicates which switch controls that luminaire. See S_a and S_b.

| ELECTRICAL PLANS MEETING ROOM | Scale 1/8 inch = 1 foot | Revised 1-1-xxxx | E-1 |

Understanding Electrical Estimating | MikeHolt.com

Counting Symbols

The purpose of counting symbols is to determine the quantity of a given electrical component or assembly that will be required on the job. This information is used to determine the quantity of items like fixtures, switches, and receptacles that will be on the job's bill of material so you can price the job. To count symbols accurately, you must be capable of reading and interpreting all drawing symbols.

When counting symbols manually, use a hand-held counter to keep track of the count. As you count a given symbol, mark it with a colored pencil, pen, or highlighter. This ensures that no symbol will be counted more than once, and that no symbol is missed in the takeoff.

Highlighters are particularly good for marking items since a single motion will color the entire symbol. This can be very helpful when you are checking to see if you have counted all of the items.

If you're using computer software to do an on-screen takeoff, use the software as instructed by the provider, but make sure to be thorough. On-screen takeoff is an excellent tool but, unlike paper, it's easy to miss an entire section of a plan that's hidden off the screen. **Figure 4–3**

Measuring to Scale

An estimate is only as accurate as the takeoff information used to produce it. One key component of a quality takeoff is measuring accurately.

Measuring consists of determining the circuit length for branch circuits, feeders, and service raceways or cables. Before you begin, verify the architectural scale listed in the drawings.

Test the scale marked on the drawing against something that you know the size of to ensure its accuracy. This is important because sometimes drawings are duplicated by a copy center or reduced in size digitally.

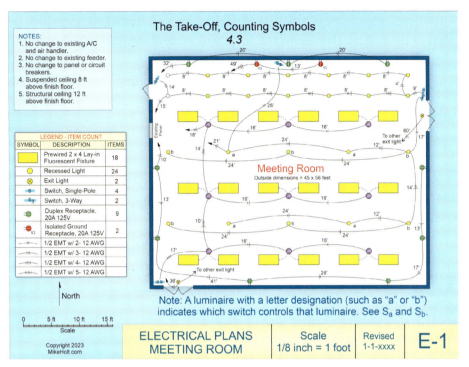

Figure 4–3

If you're using electronic drawings, don't rely on the printed scale or the settings of the file. Verify a few items before you start to ensure the scale is accurate. A little variance in the scale can result in a *huge* change in your measurements.

Scale dimensions should be noted in the drawing title block, but the scale might be different on different pages or different sections of the same page! If you are not careful, measurements can be off by as much as 100 percent.

For example, you might think you are working a ¼ in. per foot scale drawing, and it is actually a half-size drawing that is at ⅛ in. per foot scale.

Tools used to measure the circuits (on a printed drawing) include an architectural ruler, scaled-measuring tape, mechanical-measuring device, or electronic-measuring wheel. The architectural rule is fine for a few quick measurements and verifying the drawing scale.

> If the drawings don't indicate the circuit layout (most don't), you must perform this task first and then measure the circuit wiring.

Understanding Electrical Estimating | MikeHolt.com

Estimators may use a measuring tape for $\frac{1}{8}$ in. and $\frac{1}{4}$ in. scale drawings in the field, but the electronic scale wheel is the most convenient when completing an entire bid. This is because it can easily be set to multiple scales and includes a built-in counter to assist in the takeoff.

Measuring Circuits

Once you have counted symbols (fixtures, switches, and convenience receptacles), measure the branch-circuit wiring that supplies those openings.

Electronic scale wheel devices permit you to press one key to add a constant distance to the totals. But if your drops are different lengths, the constant will have to be reset. This is where computerized takeoff can save a huge amount of time.

When measuring each run, be sure to add in the drops for the overhead circuits for the switches, receptacles, and terminations at panels. Many estimators place a scaled line on the printed drawing to represent the distance of the drops so that when they come across a drop for an outlet or switch opening, they simply measure the distance from the pre-scaled line.

When measuring branch circuits, takeoff the 2-wire circuits first, the 3-wire circuits next, and then the 4-wire circuits. When measuring the circuit wiring, trace the line that represents the path you plan to take with the wiring using a colored pen or pencil. It doesn't matter what color you use, just be consistent. **Figure 4–4**

4.4 Takeoff Systems

There is no set sequence for performing the takeoff; you will develop a system that fits your personal style and needs. An exception will be those items that require a supplier's quotation because they need time to obtain accurate figures.

Whatever system you use, be sure to use the same procedures every time since consistency helps in reducing the time it takes to estimate a job, as well as reducing errors.

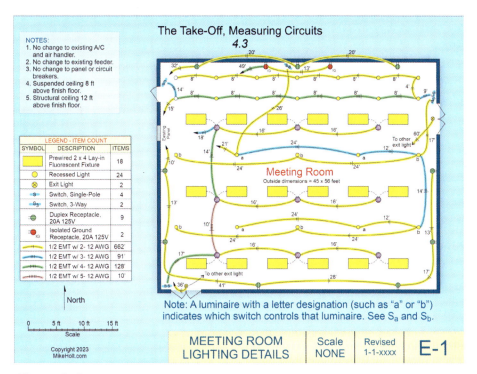

Figure 4-4

The following identifies three typical takeoff systems:

- Section at a Time
- Start with Service and End with Lighting
- Start with Lighting and End with Service

Section at a Time

Takeoff one page of the drawings at a time, or takeoff the wiring for the first floor, then all of the wiring for the second floor, and so on.

Start with Service and End with Lighting

Start the takeoff at the utility service location, continue taking off the feeders, the branch circuits, and finish by counting the lighting fixtures. This method is time consuming. It requires multiple movements between many pages of drawings and feels unnatural for most people. This style is generally not recommended, but if you have a computer-estimating system, it can work out okay.

2nd Printing

Understanding Electrical Estimating | MikeHolt.com

Start with Lighting and End with Service

This method provides an overview of the job as you count the fixtures, switches, and then convenience receptacles, which allows you to ease into the estimate. After taking off the homeruns and special circuits, you should have a good idea of the scope of the project. You will then be better prepared to deal with the more complex portions.

> Many electrical suppliers will actually perform takeoffs of your electrical plans as a part of their customer service. These takeoffs can be accurate, but be sure to review and verify the takeoff against your own. Ultimately, you are responsible for your estimate; a little mistake by the supplier could cost you the job—or a lot of money.

Lighting fixture suppliers and manufacturers often won't quote unless they have the quantities for each fixture type, so this method can be advantageous when bidding time is short.

When using the "Start with Lighting and End with Service" system, the following order is recommended:

- Count lighting fixtures
- Count switches
- Count receptacles
- Count special systems such as television, telephone, CATV, alarm, security, sound, and so on
- Count motorized and special equipment
- Count panels and service equipment
- Measure feeders and service runs
- Measure wiring for motorized and special equipment
- Measure wiring for special systems such as television, telephone, CATV, alarm, security, sound, and so on
- Measure branch-circuit wiring to outlets and related homeruns
- Measure lighting circuit wiring and related homeruns

4.5 Determining the Bill of Material

Once the takeoff is complete, the next step is to determine the bill of material, which means determining the type, size, and quantity of all material items required to complete the installation based on the items you counted during the takeoff. **Figure 4-5**

LEGEND - ITEM COUNT		
SYMBOL	DESCRIPTION	ITEMS
	Prewired 2 x 4 Lay-in Fluorescent Fixture	18
	Recessed Light	24
	Exit Light	2
S	Switch, Single-Pole	4
S₃	Switch, 3-Way	2
	Duplex Receptacle, 20A 125V	9
	Isolated Ground Receptacle, 20A 125V	2
	1/2 EMT w/ 2- 12 AWG	662'
	1/2 EMT w/ 3- 12 AWG	91'
	1/2 EMT w/ 4- 12 AWG	128'
	1/2 EMT w/ 5- 12 AWG	10'

Figure 4-5

If you are estimating manually, determining the bill of material requires the estimator to have the ability to visualize all the material items needed for each symbol.

If you don't understand the electrical wiring requirements, or don't have that visualization ability, you can't determine the bill of material, which means you can't estimate the job properly. **Figure 4-6** and **Figure 4-7**

Understanding Electrical Estimating | MikeHolt.com

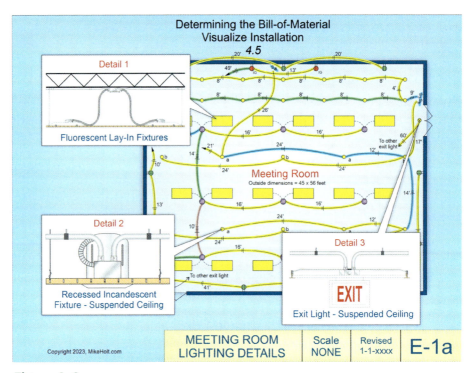

Figure 4–6

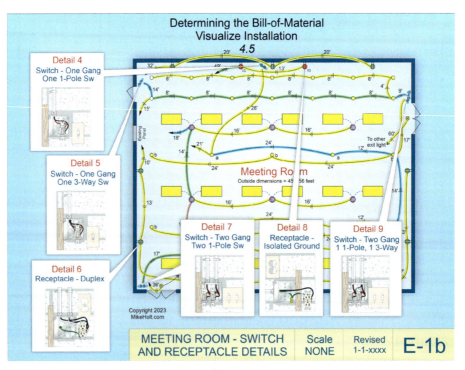

Figure 4–7

This process is labor intensive and very tedious and should only be used for very small jobs or when there isn't another option available.

If you are estimating the job with computer software, the bill of material is automatically generated from the takeoff based on the assemblies used during the count. It's still necessary for the estimator to be aware of the parts required for the assembly to be able to verify that the software is generating the correct items.

Material Spreadsheet

A best practice when doing very small manual takeoffs may be to use a spreadsheet since the bill of material and labor calculations are very simple. Save the estimating software for larger projects when the quantity of counts and variety of materials allow the computer to really save you time.

After developing the bill of material, you'll need to transfer the items and their quantities to the Price/Labor Worksheet for pricing and labor.

To extract the bill of material from a manual takeoff using a simple spreadsheet, counts can be typed into a cell that populates the total quantity of a certain piece of material in another cell automatically.

This method is simple but requires knowledge of spreadsheets and great care when working.

> **Word of Caution:** Be careful, a simple formula error in one cell or typing a count into the wrong cell can change the totals greatly.

The following spreadsheet (Meeting Room Bill of Material Spreadsheet) is based on the Meeting Room Drawing. See **Figure 4-1**.

Understanding Electrical Estimating | MikeHolt.com

Meeting Room Bill of Material														
		Boxes	½" EMT	Rings			Switches		Switch Plates		Receptacles			Blank
Description	Qty	4 × 4"	Conn.	Sq Rd	1 Gang	2 Gang	1-Pole	3-Way	1 Gang	2 Gang	Duplex	Isolated	Plates	Plates
Fixtures														
Fluorescent Lay-in (Detail 1)	18	9	18											9
Recessed (Detail 2)	24		48											
Exit (Detail 3)	2	2	4	2										
Switches														
Switch—Single Pole, 1G (Detail 4)	1	1	2		1		1		1					
Switch—3-Way, 1G (Detail 5)	1	1	2		1			1	1					
Switch—Two 1-Pole, 2G (Detail 6)	1	1	2			1	2			1				
Switch—1-Pole and 3-Way, 2G (Detail 7)	1	1	2			1	1	1		1				
Receptacles														
Receptacle 20A 125V (Detail 8)	9	9	18		9						9		9	
Receptacle IG 20A 125V (Detail 9)	2	2	4		2							2	2	
Totals	59	26	100	2	13	2	4	2	2	2	9	2	11	9

4.6 Determining Labor

After developing the bill of material, you need to transfer the items and their quantities to the Price/Labor Worksheet.

If you're using estimating software, the material quantities, pricing, and labor are automatically completed by the computer. This is fast and convenient, but still requires you to be accurate while entering counts.

A best practice may be to use a spreadsheet for very small jobs or service work with a simple labor calculation. Save the estimating software for larger projects when the quantity of counts and variety of materials allow the computer to really save you time.

Price/Labor Worksheet							
Description	Qty	Cost	U	Ext	Hr	U	Ext
Boxes							
Metal Boxes 4 × 4" Regular	26	$53.70	100		18.00	100	
EMT Set Screw Connectors ½"	100	$13.90	100		2.00	100	
Rings							
Rings, Square Round	2	$75.30	100		4.50	100	
Rings, 1-Gang	13	$43.20	100		4.50	100	
Rings, 2-Gang	2	$10.05	100		5.00	100	
Switches							
Switch—20A, 125/277V, 1-pole	4	$348.00	100		20.00	100	
Switch—20A, 125/277V, 3-Way	2	$355.30	100		25.00	100	
Plate Plastic 1-Gang Switch	2	$22.40	100		2.50	100	
Plates, Plastic 2-Gang Switch	2	$50.40	100		4.00	100	
Receptacles							
Duplex Receptacle 20A, 125V	9	$188.50	100		19.00	100	
Isolated Ground Receptacle 20A, 120V	2	$1,237.50	100		25.00	100	
Plates, Plastic 1-Gang Duplex Receptacle	11	$22.40	100		2.50	100	
Plate, Raised 4 × 4 Blank	9	$29.90	100		6.00	100	

Understanding Electrical Estimating | MikeHolt.com

Price/Labor Worksheet (continued)							
Description	Qty	Cost	U	Ext	Hr	U	Ext
Raceways							
EMT ½"	891	$15.20	100		2.25	100	
EMT Set Screw Couplings ½" (1 per 10' of EMT)	90	$15.80	100		2.00	100	
Wire							
Wire—12 THHN, Copper, 600V	2,393	$119.00	1,000		4.25	1,000	
Fixtures							
Fluorescent Lay-in	18	$58.32	1		0.75	1	
Recessed Light	24	$7.20	1		1.00	1	
Exit Fixture	2	$21.42	1		0.25	1	
Totals				$0.00			0.00

4.7 Pricing Material and Labor

Material Pricing

Pay special attention to the unit of measure that the cost reflects, such as "E" for each, "C" for 100, and "M" for 1,000.

The act of pricing consists of looking up the cost for each material item and applying it to the Price/Labor Worksheet. To save time, add the cost for each of the material items to your spreadsheet so it can automatically perform the cost extensions.

If there isn't a cost associated with a particular material item, draw a line through the cost field or highlight it so that you know later you did not omit it.

The meeting Room Drawing in **Figure 4-7** was used to complete the following pricing worksheet.

Price/Labor (Pricing) Worksheet							
Description	Qty	Cost	U	Ext	Hr	U	Ext
Boxes							
Metal Boxes 4 × 4" Regular	26	$53.70	100				
EMT Set Screw Connectors ½"	100	$13.90	100				
Rings							
Rings, Square Round	2	$75.30	100				
Rings, 1-Gang	13	$43.20	100				
Rings, 2-Gang	2	$10.05	100				
Switches							
Switch—20A, 125/277V, 1-Pole	4	$348.00	100				
Switch—20A, 125/277V, 3-Way	2	$355.30	100				
Plates, Plastic 1-Gang Switch	2	$22.40	100				
Plates, Plastic 2-Gang Switch	2	$50.40	100				
Receptacles							
Duplex Receptacle 20A, 125V	9	$188.50	100				
Isolated Ground Receptacle 20A, 120V	2	$1,237.50	100				
Plates, Plastic 1-Gang Duplex Receptacle	11	$22.40	100				
Plate, Raised 4 × 4 Blank	9	$29.90	100				
Raceways							
EMT ½"	891	$15.20	100				
EMT Set Screw Couplings ½" (1 per 10' of EMT)	90	$15.80	100				
Wire							
Wire—12 THHN, Copper, 600V	2,393	$119.00	1,000				
Fixtures							
Fluorescent Lay-in	18	$58.32	1				
Recessed Light	24	$7.20	1				
Exit Fixture	2	$21.42	1				
Totals				$0.00			0.00

Understanding Electrical Estimating | MikeHolt.com

Labor Pricing

Labor costs consists of looking up the labor unit associated with each material item and entering those values on the Price/Labor Worksheet.

To save time, add the labor units for each of the material items to your spreadsheet so the labor-hour extensions are performed automatically. The quantities from the pricing worksheet were used for the following example.

The details on exactly how to determine labor costs and use labor units in a Laboring Worksheet will be covered in the next chapter.

Laboring Worksheet							
Description	Qty	Cost	U	Ext	Hr	U	Ext
Boxes							
Metal Boxes 4 × 4" Regular	26	$53.70	100		18.00	100	
EMT Set Screw Connectors ½"	100	$13.90	100		2.00	100	
Rings							
Rings, Square Round	2	$75.30	100		4.50	100	
Rings, 1-Gang	13	$43.20	100		4.50	100	
Rings, 2-Gang	2	$10.05	100		5.00	100	
Switches							
Switch—20A, 125/277V, 1-pole	4	$348.00	100		20.00	100	
Switch—20A, 125/277V, 3-Way	2	$355.30	100		25.00	100	
Plate Plastic 1-Gang Switch	2	$22.40	100		2.50	100	
Plates, Plastic 2-Gang Switch	2	$50.40	100		4.00	100	
Receptacles							
Duplex Receptacle 20A, 125V	9	$188.50	100		19.00	100	
Isolated Ground Receptacle 20A, 120V	2	$1,237.50	100		25.00	100	
Plates, Plastic 1-Gang Duplex Receptacle	11	$22.40	100		2.50	100	
Plate, Raised 4 × 4 Blank	9	$29.90	100		6.00	100	

Laboring Worksheet (continued)

Description	Qty	Cost	U	Ext	Hr	U	Ext
Raceways							
EMT ½"	891	$15.20	100		2.25	100	
EMT Set Screw Couplings ½" (1 per 10' of EMT)	90	$15.80	100		2.00	100	
Wire							
Wire—12 THHN, Copper, 600V	2,393	$119.00	1,000		4.25	1,000	
Fixtures							
Fluorescent Lay-in	18	$58.32	1		0.75	1	
Recessed Light	24	$7.20	1		1.00	1	
Exit Fixture	2	$21.42	1		0.25	1	
Totals				$0.00			0.00

Totals

After entering the counts, material cost, and the labor-hour value for each item, you must check the totals for each worksheet page. Look for any individual numbers that look unusual and check them against the plans or calculate them manually to double check your spreadsheet formula.

If you're using estimating software, perform the same checks to make sure none of the item assemblies contained an incorrect material item or labor amount.

Understanding Electrical Estimating | MikeHolt.com

4.8 Extension

To determine (or calculate) the material cost extension for each item, divide the material cost by the unit, then multiply that value by the quantity of material items. If you're using a spreadsheet, make sure to enter individual unit quantities instead of (C) or (M) so that you can use the same formula to extend each total.

 Cost Extension Example: The total cost of 26 metal boxes that cost $53.70 per 100 (C) boxes is: $53.70/100 x 26 boxes = $13.96.

Calculate the labor-hour extension for each item by dividing the labor hours by the unit, then multiplying that value by the quantity of the material items.

If you're using a spreadsheet, make sure to enter labor individual units instead of (C) or (M) so that you can use the same formula to extend each total. Important: Have someone else double check your extensions and totals for each page. This will help you gain confidence that your material cost and labor hours are probably correct.

 Labor-Hour Extension Example: The total labor to install 26 metal boxes at 18 hours per 100 (C) boxes is: 18.00/100 x 26 boxes = 4.68 hours.

Be certain to double-check the owner-supplied equipment and/or material for accurate counts, and use your own labor units for pricing.

Extension and Totals

Description	Qty	Cost	U	Ext	Hr	U	Ext
Boxes							
Metal Boxes 4 × 4" Regular	26	$53.70	100	$13.96	18.00	100	4.68
EMT Set Screw Connectors ½"	100	$13.90	100	$13.90	2.00	100	2.00
Rings							
Rings, Square Round	2	$75.30	100	$1.51	4.50	100	0.09
Rings, 1-Gang	13	$43.20	100	$5.62	4.50	100	0.59
Rings, 2-Gang	2	$10.05	100	$0.20	5.00	100	0.10
Switches							
Switch—20A, 125/277V, 1-pole	4	$348.00	100	$13.92	20.00	100	0.80
Switch—20A, 125/277V, 3-Way	2	$355.30	100	$7.11	25.00	100	0.50
Plate Plastic 1-Gang Switch	2	$22.40	100	$0.45	2.50	100	0.05
Plates, Plastic 2-Gang Switch	2	$50.40	100	$1.01	4.00	100	0.08
Receptacles							
Duplex Receptacle 20A, 125V	9	$188.50	100	$16.97	19.00	100	1.71
Isolated Ground Receptacle 20A, 120V	2	$1,237.50	100	$24.75	25.00	100	0.50
Plates, Plastic 1-Gang Duplex Receptacle	11	$22.40	100	$2.46	2.50	100	0.28
Plate, Raised 4 × 4 Blank	9	$29.90	100	$2.69	6.00	100	0.54
Raceways							
EMT ½"	891	$15.20	100	$135.43	2.25	100	20.05
EMT Set Screw Couplings ½" (1 per 10' of EMT)	90	$15.80	100	$14.22	2.00	100	1.80
Wire							
Wire—12 THHN, Copper, 600V	2,393	$119.00	1000	$284.77	4.25	1000	10.17
Fixtures							
Fluorescent Lay-in	18	$58.32	1	$1,049.76	0.75	1	13.50
Recessed Light	24	$7.20	1	$172.80	1.00	1	24.00
Exit Fixture	2	$21.42	1	$42.84	0.25	1	0.50
Totals				$1,804.37			81.94

Understanding Electrical Estimating | MikeHolt.com

4.9 Historical Data

It's no secret that an estimator's best friend is historical data, and what makes this data most effective is accurate record keeping.

As your business grows and you've completed and reconciled more and more jobs, those file folders that you've been keeping for each job estimate establish a track record of costs, profits, and/or losses for each job.

This working job history is an invaluable resource when estimating new work that is similar to work that you've already done. You can look back at this data to see what it took to complete a particular job (or aspect of a job) and make any adjustments deemed necessary to labor units or material assemblies to ensure a more accurate bid.

Final Thoughts

So far you have reviewed what estimating is in Chapter 1, what makes a good estimator in Chapter 2, the estimating process in Chapter 3, and the takeoff here in Chapter 4.

You saw that preparing an estimate requires performing specific steps in a specific order, that precision is a critical component of an accurate estimate, and that using a computer to assist you in this process is almost mandatory. In the next chapter we will dive deeper into how to determine labor costs.

Use the information you learned in this chapter to answer the following questions.

Chapter 4—Review Questions

4.1 Introduction

1. Part of the science of estimating is to accurately determine how many of each part and each task must be performed so that you can calculate an accurate labor and material budget. This process is called the____.

    (a) design stage
    (b) planning stage
    (c) comparison stage
    (d) takeoff

4.2 The Takeoff Sequence

2. The list of steps in the takeoff sequence to be reviewed for an accurate takeoff includes,____.

    (a) understanding the scope
    (b) organizing project documents
    (c) visiting the jobsite
    (d) all of these

3. The scope of work describes the work that needs to be done ____.

    (a) for a project
    (b) within a certain time frame
    (c) in house
    (d) by subcontractors

4. Your first step in preparing for a takeoff is to make sure to obtain a complete set of drawings including the ____.

    (a) site plans
    (b) architectural plans
    (c) floor plans
    (d) all of these

5. The Site Plan is typically identified by the letter ____ preceding the page numbers.

    (a) A
    (b) B
    (c) C
    (d) S

6. The site plans contain the civil engineering portion of the project, and show where the ____ are located.

    (a) parking lot lights
    (b) landscape lights
    (c) utility connections
    (d) all of these

7. The architectural plan is typically identified by the letter ____ (Architectural) preceding the page numbers.

    (a) A
    (b) B
    (c) C
    (d) S

8. Architectural drawings will include information such as building and structural materials, wall cross-sections and dimensions, wall and floor finishes, and ____.

    (a) elevator locations
    (b) building elevations
    (c) emergency egress
    (d) job trailer locations

9. Floor plans are typically identified by the letter(s) ____.

    (a)   FP
    (b)   M, P, and E
    (c)   F
    (d)   any of these

10. Plans specifications are designed to simplify the task of ____, and to make sure all bidders are providing the same product for the bid price.

    (a)   installing equipment
    (b)   bidding a job
    (c)   interpreting the drawings
    (d)   scheduling the job

11. Construction project specifications are typically organized by divisions defined by the Construction Specification Institute (CSI). The current system contains ____ divisions specific to the electrical trade.

    (a)   five
    (b)   eight
    (c)   48
    (d)   60

12. Before counting items on the plan, review all ____ and identify easily-overlooked items. Underline, circle, or highlight important and/or unusual items that can affect the estimate.

    (a)   plan and specifications pages
    (b)   electrical codes
    (c)   fire codes
    (d)   local ordinances

13. If you don't understand something in the drawings or specifications, you might have the tendency to delay the estimate until the last minute. This will result in ____.

    (a)   losing a customer
    (b)   a late bid
    (c)   losing the job
    (d)   being terminated

Understanding Electrical Estimating | MikeHolt.com

4.3 The Takeoff

14. A proper takeoff ensures there will be little need to refer to the _____ to complete the estimate.

   (a) architect
   (b) drawings or specifications
   (c) customer
   (d) general contractor

15. When you do a manual takeoff on paper or digital plans, follow a specific _____ to identify those items taken off.

   (a) routine
   (b) schedule
   (c) color code
   (d) pattern

16. When you have finished the takeoff, your drawings should be a colored representation of the _____ that needs to be installed.

   (a) fire suppression system
   (b) electrical work
   (c) fire alarm and security system
   (d) ADA requirements

17. The purpose of counting symbols during takeoff is to determine the _____ of a given electrical component or assembly that will be required on the job.

   (a) type
   (b) size
   (c) rating
   (d) quantity

18. One key component of a quality takeoff is measuring accurately. Measuring consists of determining the circuit length for _____ or cables.

   (a) branch-circuits
   (b) feeders
   (c) service raceways
   (d) all of these

19. When doing the takeoff and measuring each circuit run, be sure to add in the drops for the overhead circuits for the ____.

    (a)   switches
    (b)   receptacles
    (c)   terminations at panels
    (d)   all of these

4.4 Takeoff Systems

20. There are ____ typical takeoff systems.

    (a)   two
    (b)   three
    (c)   four
    (d)   many

21. Performing a takeoff one page of the drawings at a time, or takeoff the wiring for the first floor, then all of the wiring for the second floor, and so on describes the ____ system.

    (a)   Section-at-a-Time
    (b)   Beginning-to-End
    (c)   End-to-Beginning
    (d)   Long Method

4.5 Determining the Bill of Material

22. Once the takeoff is complete, the next step is to determine the bill of material, which means determining the ____ of all material items required to complete the installation.

    (a)   type
    (b)   size
    (c)   quantity
    (d)   all of these

Understanding Electrical Estimating | MikeHolt.com

23. If you are estimating manually, determining the bill of material requires the estimator to have the ability to visualize all the ____ needed for each symbol.

(a) tools
(b) skill
(c) material items
(d) installation time

4.6 Determining Labor

24. If you're using estimating software, the material quantities, pricing, and ____ are automatically completed by the computer.

(a) delivery schedule
(b) installation time
(c) labor
(d) weight

4.7 Pricing Material and Labor

25. After entering the counts, material cost, and the ____ for each item, you must check the totals for each worksheet page.

(a) sales tax
(b) overhead
(c) labor-hour value
(d) rental fees

4.8 Extension

26. To determine (or calculate) the material cost extension for each item, divide the material cost by the unit, then ____ the quantity of material items.

(a) add that value to
(b) subtract that value from
(c) divide that value by
(d) multiply that value by

4.9 Historical Data

27. It's no secret that an estimator's best friend is historical data, and what makes this data most effective is _____ record keeping.

    (a)   a high volume of work
    (b)   accurate record keeping
    (c)   time and material jobs
    (d)   not using subcontractors

28. As you've completed and reconciled more and more jobs, those file folders that you've been keeping for each job estimate creates historical data that establishes a track record of _____ for each job.

    (a)   costs
    (b)   profits
    (c)   losses
    (d)   all of these

Understanding Electrical Estimating | MikeHolt.com

Notes...

2nd Printing

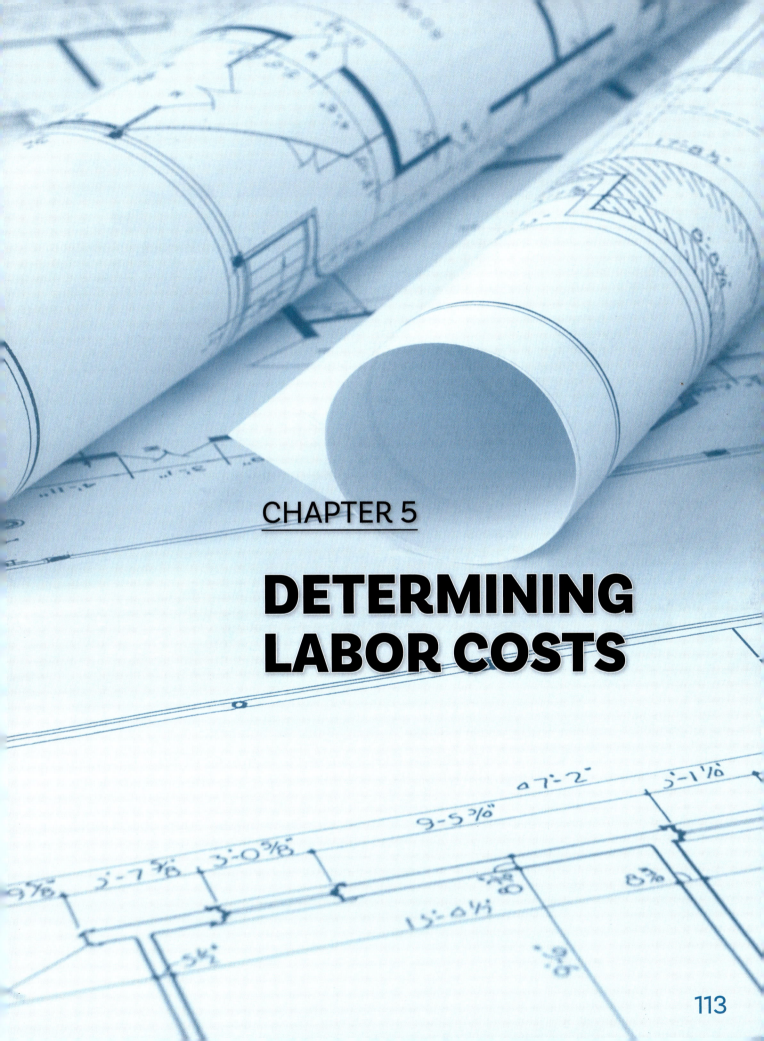

CHAPTER 5

DETERMINING LABOR COSTS

5.1 Introduction

When you do an electrical estimate, two of the major cost components of the job you will need to determine include material/equipment and labor. The labor component is where the estimate is most likely to go wrong, and where errors can do the greatest damage to the project.

To estimate labor requirements, you start with standard labor-unit guides that tell you how many labor hours it should take to do a certain task under "typical" job conditions. For example, 1 Recess can = 1 hour to install.

Once we know the hours, we calculate the total labor then multiply the total hours by the cost per hour for labor.

Here's what we will consider in determining labor costs:

5.2   **Basis of a Labor Unit**
5.3   **Expressing Labor Units**
5.4   **Components of a Labor Unit**
5.5   **Labor-Unit Manuals**
5.6   **Adjusting Labor Units**
5.7   **Labor Unit Variables**

5.2 Basis of a Labor Unit

A labor unit represents the approximate amount of time required to install an electrical product, component, or piece of equipment. Labor units are based on the assumption that a skilled electrician is completing the task under a *specific* set of installation conditions, and that the appropriate tools and supervision are available.

Labor is based on:

- Project Conditions
- Site Conditions

Project Conditions

The following typical project considerations should be used for the purposes of estimating using standard labor units:

- Up to three floors
- 20,000 to 100,000 square feet per floor
- Rectangular or square floor plan
- Installation not more than 20 feet above a solid floor or grade
- Standard workday/week
- No more than 100 qualified electricians on the job
- Metropolitan area, outside of a controlled access area
- Single building, facility, or activity
- Utilities-supplied power
- New-listed material

Site Conditions

The following typical site considerations should be used for the purposes of estimating using labor units:

- Adequate security for material and tool storage
- All electrical material furnished by electrical contractor
- All new material and new construction
- Materials are readily available with minimal lead time for special items
- Complete drawings and specifications are provided with engineering and a well-coordinated design
- High-reach, lift, and/or excavation equipment is supplied by others
- Standard building type, design, and construction
- Few interruptions or delays
- Minimal quantity and magnitude of change orders
- Minimum temperature of 35°F, maximum temperature of 88°F, and 50 percent relative humidity

- Optimal job coordination of all trades
- Overall job progress based on a realistic predetermined project schedule
- Sufficient supply of skilled labor and qualified journeymen electricians

Labor units must be adjusted for management skill and any variable conditions on the jobsite. The methods of adjusting labor units are discussed later in this chapter.

5.3 Expressing Labor Units

> You might think that 11 minutes to install a duplex receptacle is way too much time, and you will never win a job if you use labor units, but that is really not the case. Once you understand what the labor unit is made of it will all make sense.

A labor unit is a representation of the amount of time that it is expected to take to install a material in a normal job situation.

For example, if a receptacle is listed as 18/C, it means that it will take 18 hours to install one-hundred receptacles. If #12 THHN is listed as 4.25/M, it means that it will take 4.25 hours to install one-thousand feet of THHN.

The reason labor hours are expressed in decimal form is to make them easy to calculate rather than having to work with hours and minutes individually.

Labor Calculation Example: What is the labor to install a receptacle is listed as 18/C?

100 Receptacles = 18 hours
18 Hours/100 = 0.18 hours each
60 Minutes × 0.18 Hours Each = 11 minutes

Answer: 11 min per receptacle

Understanding Electrical Estimating | Mike Holt Enterprises

Calculating Labor

It's important to consider work experience when calculating labor because it allows you to foresee the pitfalls of particular types of jobs that could impact the efficiency of your employees. Many electrical contractors estimate a job based on how long they think it will take them to do it, here are other factors that must be considered:

- Organizational Experience
- Company Experience
- Personal Experience

Organizational Experience

Factors, such as amount of supervision required, availability of qualified employees, job layout, handling of tools and material, nonproductive time, and job conditions, all influence the efficiency of employees on a job. Rarely will these numbers line up with the amount of time it would take if you personally could install every piece of material on a project.

Company Experience

Experience, for a contracting company, exists in the records of past jobs. If they are like the one you are estimating, you can carry over much of the information to the new job.

Personal Experience

Personal experience provides a "feel" for what it takes to do a job. Keep in mind that one's memory has a way of changing the "facts" over time. As a result, you should use personal experience to *check* your estimated labor requirements, not to *determine* them.

The approach of using labor units takes more time than trying to guess how long it will take to do the job, but doing so reduces the likelihood of errors and oversights. Just one error can turn a

Understanding Electrical Estimating | MikeHolt.com

profit-promising job into a money-losing job. Use your personal experience as a guide—but remember that it's only *one* factor used to estimate a job.

> Differences in how labor hours are estimated are one of the primary reasons there is such a variation in pricing between electrical contractors.

Effect of Experience

How many labor hours do you think it will take to complete the wiring for the Meeting Room Drawing? **Figure 5-1**

I have asked over 1,000 master electricians in my classes to estimate the labor hours required to rough in and trim the meeting room. The answers range from a low of 40 hours to over 200 hours. If you like, show the plan to five electricians and ask them what they think and you will see what I mean.

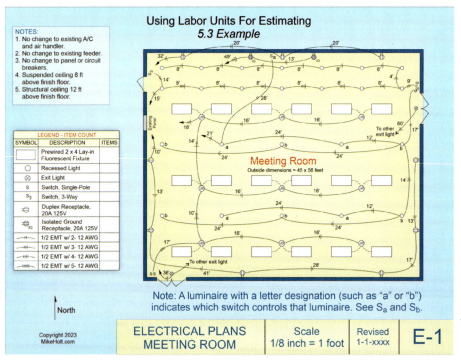

Figure 5-1

Based on the following labor units, the estimated labor hours for the Meeting Room will be 82.84 hours (see the following table).

Some electrical contractors will be more efficient and organized and complete the project in less time, whereas other electrical contractors are so disorganized that they will be lucky to finish it in less than 125 hours.

Meeting Room Labor Units					
Description	Qty	Hrs	Unit	Ext Hrs	Calculation
Boxes					
Metal Boxes 4 × 4" Regular	30	18.00	C/100	5.40	18 hr/100 × 30
Rings					
Rings, Square Round	6	4.50	C/100	0.27	4.50 hr/100 × 6
Rings, 1-Gang	13	4.50	C/100	0.59	4.50 hr/100 × 13
Rings, 2-Gang	2	5.00	C/100	0.10	5 hr/100 × 2
Switches					
Switch—20A, 125/277V, 1-Pole	4	20.00	C/100	0.80	20 hr/100 × 4
Switch—20A, 125/277V, 3-Way	2	25.00	C/100	0.50	25 hr/100 × 2
Receptacles					
Duplex Receptacle 20A, 125V	9	19.00	C/100	1.71	19 hr/100 × 9
Isolated Ground Receptacle 20A, 120V	2	0.25	E/Each	0.50	0.25 hr × 2
Plates					
Plates, Plastic 1-Gang Switch	2	2.50	C/100	0.05	2.50 hr/100 × 2
Plates, Plastic 2-Gang Switch	2	4.00	C/100	0.08	4 hr/100 × 2
Plates, Plastic 1-Gang Duplex Receptacle	11	2.50	C/100	0.28	2.50 hr/100 × 11
Plates, Raised 4 × 4" Blank	9	6.00	C/100	0.54	6 hr/100 × 9
Raceway					
EMT ½"	891	2.25	C/100	20.05	2.25 hr/100 × 891
EMT Set Screw Connectors ½"	100	2.00	C/100	2.00	2 hr/100 × 100
EMT Set Screw Couplings ½"	90	2.00	C/100	1.80	2 hr/100 × 90
Wire					

Meeting Room Labor Units (continued)					
Description	**Qty**	**Hrs**	**Unit**	**Ext Hrs**	**Calculation**
Wire—12 THHN, Copper, 600V	2,393	4.25	M/1,000	10.17	4.25 hr/1000 × 2,393
Fixtures					
4' Fluorescent Lay-In, 2 Lamps, 120V	18	0.75	E/Each	13.50	0.75 hr × 18
Recessed Fixture	24	1.00	E/Each	24.00	1 hr × 24
Exit Fixture	2	0.25	E/Each	0.50	0.25 hr × 2
Total Labor-Unit Hours				82.84	

5.4 Components of a Labor Unit

A labor unit has six major components: **Figure 5-2**

- Installation
- Job Layout
- Material Handling and Cleanup
- Nonproductive Labor
- Supervision
- Tool Handling and Safety
- Not Included in a Labor Unit

Installation

The actual installation time only represents about 50 percent of the labor unit. It includes the physical time it should take to install boxes, conduit, fittings, wiring devices, fixtures, switchgear, disconnects, panels, breakers, and so on. Be sure you always provide the proper tools so the installation can be completed in the most efficient manner.

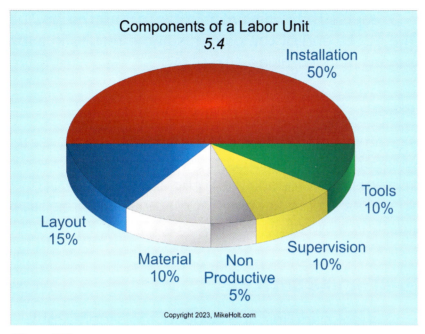

Figure 5–2

Job Layout

The layout of the work represents 15 percent of the labor unit. It includes measuring and determining the type, size, and location of the raceways, wire, cables, boxes, circuits, fixtures, and so on.

Material Handling and Cleanup

Material handling and cleanup represents 10 percent of the labor unit. Do not forget you must unpack, receive, count, unload, store material, and dispose of the packing containers in which the items were shipped.

Nonproductive Labor

All jobs include nonproductive labor, which should be managed so as not to exceed 5 percent of the labor unit.

Be careful of long breaks and early quitting-times which are often linked with late-starting times. You know how it goes: two guys look at their watches, one watch indicates 8:00 a.m., and the other shows

Understanding Electrical Estimating | MikeHolt.com

7:55 a.m. Of course, they wait five minutes to start the job. The opposite is true at the end of the day. This game results in a loss of 10 minutes a day per electrician.

Supervision

Supervision represents 10 percent of the labor unit. It includes reviewing the drawings and specifications, ordering material, working out installation problems, coordinating with other trades and subcontractors, inspection tours, record keeping for material, job progress reports, time cards, and a ton of other things.

Tool Handling and Safety

The management, handling, and layout of tools represent 10 percent of the labor unit. Somebody must receive, store, move, set up, remove, and clean the tools! Another item that may seem inconsequential but can really impact your bid is safety. Be sure to include any and all safety and personal protective equipment (PPE) required by the bid documents. Overlooking this on the estimate can really add up on longer jobs.

Not Included in a Labor Unit

Labor units include all the expected labor to install a unit of material, but they do not include many of the other common causes of additional labor on a project.

Some examples of time not accounted for in a labor unit are listed below. It's important to include every single detail when building an estimate or writing a change order, or the costs will come out of your profit.

Factors that are *not* included in a labor unit are:

- Assembly of fixtures or equipment supplied by others
- Special or additional supervision
- Difficult site access (like security at a jail or remote parking)

- Cutting holes or openings
- Excavation, drilling, or blasting
- Heavy equipment or crane operators' time
- Hoisting material and equipment above three floors
- Maintenance of temporary equipment
- Painting of conduits
- Patching or painting
- Testing or welding
- Sealing fire-rated penetrations

Labor Units for Unusual Tasks

There will be times when you must determine the amount of labor needed for a task that you have absolutely no idea how to approach. What you need to do is break the task down into as many small individual labor segments as possible.

Try to establish a labor unit for each segment by comparing the individual segments to a similar task that you do have a labor unit for. If all else fails, make an educated guess based on experience and prior knowledge.

If your employees are not familiar with a particular type of work, the labor required to manage, install, and troubleshoot that system will be significantly increased.

5.5 Labor-Unit Manuals

You must purchase a comprehensive labor-unit manual that contains at least 10,000 labor units. Excellent labor-unit manuals are available from many sources. Be sure to stick to labor units shown in a single manual for the entire job because they are developed in a coordinated manner.

There is no perfect set of labor units that can be applied to *all* jobs by *all* electrical contractors. With experience and historical data, you will develop techniques to help you adjust the labor units so they represent your productivity under specific job conditions.

Understanding Electrical Estimating | MikeHolt.com

5.6 Adjusting Labor Units

You won't actually develop your own labor units. You will, however, develop a "labor-unit adjustment" you will apply to adjust the labor units you are using. To determine your labor-unit adjustments, compare the estimated hours of a job against the actual number of hours it took.

After tracking a few jobs, you will learn what your adjustment is for the next job, based on the labor units that you are using.

> If you do not manage your job properly, your actual labor hours will likely exceed the estimate. If your labor-unit adjustment reflects your inefficiency, your bids will not be as competitive as they can be.

When adjusting labor units make sure to consider the following:

- Being Competitive
- Project Management
- Labor Skill Level
- Labor Training
- Labor Experience
- Material and Tools
- Supervision
- Other Bidders

Being Competitive

Productivity in the installation of electrical equipment is affected by many factors, and the most significant is project management. If the actual labor exceeds the estimate, the primary cause is usually a deficiency in project management.

Understanding Electrical Estimating | Mike Holt Enterprises

This is because management determines the labor budget, level of supervision, and whether the labor force is skilled and motivated enough to be sufficiently productive. Management is also responsible for having the proper tools and material on the job at the right time.

Project Management

The estimate must provide the estimated labor hour/cost budget for each phase of the job (slab, rough in, and trim). With this information, the electricians in the field have a basis to know how many hours it should take to complete a given portion of the project so it can be managed to the expectation of the estimator.

If no one knows how long it should take to complete a project, you will never know if your labor is productive, and you will not be able to move the project to completion in a profitable manner. It is a good idea for your project management team to know what the labor budget is and to assign tasks to your employees that they like to do and at which they excel. They will be happier, more productive, and more likely to meet your labor estimate.

Labor Skill Level

Labor units assume that highly trained, skilled, and motivated electricians are completing the task—and your customers expect as much.

Some electrical contractors "save money" by using an unskilled and unmotivated labor force (which is less productive and more prone to costly errors), while other electrical contractors cultivate a highly skilled and motivated team that will get the job done.

The labor cost of any on the job training (OJT) is your responsibility and those costs should not be passed on to your customers. The skill and motivation of your labor force will affect your labor productivity. You know the saying, "You get what you pay for."

> Trying to save money by using unskilled, unmotivated labor will actually cost you money, not save it.

Labor Training

Trained, skilled, and motivated electricians will complete work faster, period! Be sure your employees are properly trained in advance for all aspects of their job including safety, the proper use of tools, the *NEC*, and efficient work practices.

The investment in training is offset by increased labor productivity, reduced down-time due to accidents or injuries, and reduced callbacks or rework.

Labor Experience

With experience, workers can complete a project more quickly. If you estimate jobs with which you have experience, you should have a more competitive labor unit, as opposed to jobs with which you have little or no experience.

One example of this concept in action is in tract housing. An experienced electrical contractor can beat standard unadjusted labor units by as much as 40 percent and still make money, whereas a commercial electrical contractor (having never done houses) will be lucky to break even, without any labor-unit adjustment.

Material and Tools

To complete a project efficiently, you must have the material and tools, and all pertinent information, on the job when they are needed.

If they are not, then your labor force will be wasting your money trying to find something to do while they are waiting. Whose fault is this? Remember, labor units are based on a skilled electrician utilizing the most current labor-saving tools. If you do not provide proper tools on time and training on the safe use of those tools, your labor force cannot be as productive.

Make sure the tools are always properly maintained and are in a safe working condition.

Supervision

A qualified management team can make or break a job. Your managers need to follow the estimate, stay on schedule, and coordinate with other trades throughout the job. The best field team is only as good as the manager running the job.

Other Bidders

Labor rates are unique to each company and team. It does not help you to know the labor units your competitors use because your management style, organizational strengths and weaknesses, and the skill of your labor force are all unique to your company.

To be competitive, you must continue to strive to improve efficiency and effectiveness as an electrical contractor. Do not worry about your competitors, you have enough problems of your own to work on!

5.7 Labor Unit Variables

There are other factors that also impact a labor unit. Identical electrical material used in different types of buildings and projects may require either more or less labor to install than the average amount of labor for a given part.

Data from a labor-unit manual must be adjusted to fit the job conditions that you are dealing with. Some job variables can be anticipated and controlled, while others must be accepted as a cost of doing business.

> Remember—there isn't a set of labor units that fits every job.

The adjustment factors that we will be discussing are only a suggested guide. You must keep historical information on past jobs to develop your own adjustments. Keep in mind that you may only have a few of these variables on any one job. Variables with significant impact include:

- Building Complexity
- Change Orders
- Project Management
- Jobsite Factors

Building Complexity

A complex building design can cause confusion and often requires greater supervision, so you need to be alert to this condition. For example, it takes more time to run 100 ft of trade size $^3/_4$ EMT in an existing research laboratory than it does to run it down the wall of an unfinished warehouse.

Different material used to build the same building may also have a bearing on how long it takes to install material. For example, installing a lighting box on a wood-framed ceiling member is much easier than installing the same box on a metal-framed ceiling. The following are building complexity factors that must be considered:

- Floor Conditions
- Hoisting Restrictions
- Working Height
- Multistory Single-Floor Level Adjustment
- Multi-Story Entire Building Adjustment

> "Many times, on larger jobs, general labor is provided by the developer or general contractor. Their sole task is to maintain a clean jobsite. Make sure to indicate or protect what isn't trash or you may get to buy more!

Floor Conditions

If the floor area is covered with sheets of plywood, wood, garbage, or even rainwater, you can bet that it is going to take your staff more time to complete the installation.

Some general contractors require the subcontractors to clean up after themselves so that the next trade has a clean working area, whereas other general contractors let this issue resolve itself between the subcontractors. Not only is this a labor item on the bid, but it may also impact the efficiency of your crew.

2nd Printing

Hoisting Restrictions

In some high-rise buildings, elevators or cranes can only be used to transport construction material during certain hours of the day, so be sure to coordinate the movement of material and tools so that you do not have electricians standing around waiting for them.

Some projects will require that material be moved only during off-hours, or that you schedule your time for crane or buck hoist use in advance. Additional costs for premium time need to be included in your bid if this will cause you to work outside normal hours.

Working Height

Labor units are based on buildings and projects with up to three floors above grade or street level. As the number and height of floors increase, there is an increase in the number of labor hours needed to install and move the same equipment, material, tools.

In addition, the need to wait for the lifts at the start of the day, end of the day, breaks, lunch, charging time, and so on, increases the number of labor hours that will be required.

Multistory Single-Floor Level Adjustment

Add one percent for the single floor level you are working on. For example, if you are doing a build-out on the ninth floor, increase your total labor by nine percent.

Note: NECAnet.org has a research report entitled, *The Effect of Multi-Story Buildings on Productivity.*

Multistory Entire Building Adjustment

When wiring the entire building, use the following table for adjustment factors that apply to the total building labor hours for buildings with repetitive floor drawings.

Understanding Electrical Estimating | MikeHolt.com

Multistory Building Labor Adjustments	
1 to 2 Floors	0%
3 to 6 Floors	1%
7 to 8 Floors	2%
9 to 14 Floors	5%
15 to 19 Floors	7%
20 to 30 Floors	13%

Change Orders

Jobs are rarely completed as originally planned; revisions to the electrical system are often required to accommodate changes in the building design, or to accommodate a change in the owner's needs.

Change orders often result in a delay in the job schedule for all trades, which in itself can decrease the labor productivity of your staff. Because change orders often affect the planning or scheduling of work, those in the field sometimes develop a negative work ethic and unfavorable worker attitude toward the project that hinders productivity.

> Be sure that any and all change orders are in writing and signed by someone who is authorized to approve any additional costs incurred as a result of the change(s).

In addition, there are other monetary factors you should consider when dealing with change orders, which include increased overhead cost, interruption of job flow, the effect on labor when compressing the job schedule, overtime, revisions to as-built drawings, increased project management cost, and possible restocking charges from your suppliers for returned items. If the schedule is delayed, there are other unexpected costs, such as increased financing cost, storage cost, supervision cost, and so on, which must be recovered.

There are no specific labor adjustments you can add to a job for anticipated change orders. The best you can do is be aware of the impact on the estimated job labor.

You might need to add additional labor when pricing the change order to compensate for the loss in productivity it causes to the original labor estimate. Adding scope can interrupt work flow and cause otherwise productive employees to be much less productive.

Note: NECAnet.org has a research report entitled, *Impact of Change Orders on Labor Efficiency for Electrical Construction.*

Project Management

Labor units are based on the effective coordination and management of the project by the contractor or construction manager. If the project is not managed effectively by the contractor, productivity losses will occur.

Losses can occur because of:

- An accelerated construction schedule
- Excessive change orders
- Material furnished by the owner
- Overtime to maintain the construction schedule
- Poor coordination of subcontractors
- Redesign of any part of a project after construction has started
- Starting construction without complete or coordinated construction drawings

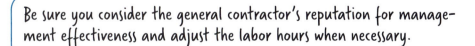

Be sure you consider the general contractor's reputation for management effectiveness and adjust the labor hours when necessary.

Jobsite Factors

Labor units are based on typical job locations that do not include any unusual problems. When a project location creates unusual material and tool handling issues, any type of physical or administrative obstructions, productivity losses must be considered. Some of the

Understanding Electrical Estimating | MikeHolt.com

abnormal conditions that may cause productivity losses are in the sections that follow, but productivity losses due to abnormal job conditions must be determined by judgment, logic, and common sense.

Out-of-Town Work

Travel and remote jobsites create a variety of challenges. Be careful when estimating the labor requirements for an out-of-town job.

If the job is remote from the office, the challenge for the office to ensure that the job is managed effectively increases. Sometimes a job located in a remote location is forgotten or ignored by the electrical contractor, and that could have disastrous results.

Be careful when estimating the labor requirements for an out-of-town job that requires you to hire local electricians for a temporary period of time. Will the pay scale be higher than it is in your immediate area? How productive or loyal do you think the workers will be? For out-of-town work, remember to consider items such as:

- Local pay scale
- Productivity and loyalty of short-term employees
- Travel time to the jobsite
- Lodging and other related costs for your staff

TIP! Make it a point to regularly visit your jobsites in person. Employees will stay more focused on production if they know you will be dropping in to check on them.

Small Jobs

Smaller jobs require a much higher labor unit because they have the same base costs as a large job, but without the volume of work to offset the costs. There is no standard adjustment factor for this type of situation, so track your labor on each job to see what pattern develops.

Understanding Electrical Estimating | Mike Holt Enterprises

Qualified Personnel

Labor units are based on having an adequate supply of qualified electricians. Not having them results in a loss of productivity that must be taken into consideration during the estimating process. It is impossible to precisely determine that loss, but an attempt must be made based on experience, judgment, and common sense.

Employee Attitude

Your attitude toward your employees determines turnover and productivity rates. If you treat them well, pay fairly, provide benefits, and pay for continuing education, you will have dedicated employees who will do all they can to take care of you and your customers.

Motivation

A well-paid, motivated, qualified, highly trained, and experienced electrician will always be more productive than an employee who feels cheated, does not care about the success of your business, and does not feel like part of the team.

If you do not have motivated, skilled, and experienced electricians, the ones you do have will need extra supervision. Poorly skilled labor results in an increase in costs to correct violations and fix mistakes.

Your hiring policy will determine the quality of your employees and their attitude, but how you treat them will determine how long they will stay and how productive they will be.

Training

A continuously trained labor force will always be more efficient and productive than an unskilled force. Your investment in continuing education will result in increased labor productivity.

Understanding Electrical Estimating | MikeHolt.com

Do you have a training program to teach your employees how to be more productive? What about people skills so they understand how to treat each other, the other trades, and customers? If you fail an inspection, do you have a review process so that all staff members know what was wrong, so the same mistake is not repeated?

Safety training decreases the likelihood of an accident. Any accident drives costs up due to downtime and increased insurance costs. It also shows your employees that you are concerned for them, and that will increase production.

Preassembled Equipment

Whenever possible, purchase preassembled equipment or equipment that is installer-friendly. Equipment that's not preassembled will cost you more by the time you spend money on the labor to put it together.

There's never enough time to complete a project, and there's never enough labor available. Purchasing materials that are easier to install will allow your team to move on to the next part of the project without bogging down skilled employees with tedious tasks better done at a factory.

Examples of preassembled equipment include ordering lay-in fixtures with wire connectors already installed, or ordering feeder conductor pulls in the correct color and length already on the same reel. The cost might be slightly greater, but the labor savings will exceed the increased material cost.

Embedded Wiring

When installing wiring systems such as boxes and raceway systems in concrete or masonry portions of a building, you need to realize that they often require significantly more labor as compared to installing the same wiring concealed in a drywall partition.

Consider applying the following adjustments for concealed wiring:

Embedded Wiring Labor Adjustments	
Boxes/raceways in walls	50%
Boxes/raceways in columns	100%

Exposed Wiring

Installing exposed wiring methods such as boxes and raceways requires more installation time in order to do nice offsets and ensure that the pipe is installed parallel and level along the building lines. Where multiple raceways are run next to each other, each must be carefully bent so they are run symmetrically.

Consider applying the following labor adjustments to that portion of the wiring method that will be exposed:

Exposed Wiring Labor Adjustments	
Boxes	10%
Raceways	20%

Unusual Tasks

Sometimes you have no clue how to approach an installation. Break unusual tasks down into as many small individual labor segments as possible and establish a labor unit by comparing them to something that you already have a labor unit for. This process will help you develop an accurate feel for the labor for the task. Once you have completed the work, make sure to go back and update the labor unit to reflect the actual installation time.

Ladder Work

Any portion of a job that requires working on a ladder will result in an increase in labor as compared to a job at grade level. Working is more difficult and tiring on a ladder, and there is an increased risk of injury from falls.

The following labor-unit adjustments for ladder work should be considered for any portion of the job that is not at grade level.

Understanding Electrical Estimating | MikeHolt.com

Ladder Labor-Unit Adjustments	
12 ft	3%
13 ft	5%
14 ft	8%
15 ft	10%
16 ft	13%
17 ft	16%
18 ft	19%
19 ft	22%
20 ft	25%

Scaffold Work

If you are performing work from a scaffold, you need to consider the labor required to set up, move, and dismantle it. Do not forget you have to somehow get tools and material up to the working platform. Then before the scaffold can be moved, all tools, equipment, and material must be brought back down.

If in moving the scaffold, you encounter a large obstruction (like a doorway), it might have to be disassembled and reassembled. For safety and efficiency, you will need one electrician at the bottom of the scaffold at all times.

How much do you increase the labor unit for work performed on a scaffold? This is a tough one, but figure at least a 40 to 50 percent increase in labor units, plus the time to wrestle with it (setup time, take-down, and the time needed to return the scaffold).

If the work can be performed from motorized platform lifts, this adjustment can be significantly reduced.

Productivity

Proper job management ensures a well-trained and motivated quality workforce that has the material, tools, and information needed to get the job done right the first time with the least amount of effort. If properly trained, equipped, and motivated, your workforce will be content and proud to work for your company—that means they will give their best.

If you (the manager or owner) are not organized, you can be sure that those below you are not organized either, and you will have difficulty competing in today's market.

The most efficient way to have a productive labor force is for them to be happy. Of course, everybody wants a bigger paycheck, but that is not all there is to being happy. What people desire is to feel valued, and believe they are part of something special.

Be sure your management staff follows your lead. Do not forget to provide supervisory training for them in all aspects of their responsibility including people skills, job budgeting, project management, and time management.

Make sure you have a high level of communication from the office to the on-site supervisor about the project at hand, and about how the job was estimated. Be sure you have meetings between the office and field personnel to review job progress on a regular basis.

Here are a few tips for success on the jobsite:

- Hire the right people
- Pay them fairly and provide benefits
- Educate both field and management staff
- Communicate, communicate, communicate
- Let them know they're important

Planning Material Orders

Planning your material orders is critical to ensure the electricians on the job are not held up due to material shortages. There are hundreds of minor items your workers can run out of. Any one of them can stop a job in its tracks and cost you money while someone makes a parts run.

Remember, if the material is not delivered to the job on time, you will be losing money you did not need to lose. Running out of material on a job destroys continuity and motivation on the job—not to mention the cost of inefficiency.

Overtime

Labor units are based on normal work schedules of 8 daylight hours per day, five days per week, and 40 total hours per week, with a minimum amount of overtime once or twice a month. When overtime is required for any reason, there is a substantial loss of productivity during the overtime hours worked.

As overtime increases in magnitude and duration, productivity losses also increase. Overtime interrupts established life patterns and causes fatigue, reduced motivation, and lower productivity. Workers have a tendency to forget safety procedures, which can result in serious accidents and possible fatalities. Consider the following adjustments:

Overtime Adjustments	
Six 8-Hour Days	
One Week	+ 15% for the 6th Day
Every Week	+ 15% All Labor for Week
Saturdays and Sundays after Five Days	
One Weekend	+ 30% for Weekend Hours
Every Weekend	+ 30% All Labor for week
Extended Regular Hours	
Six 10-hour Days	+ 18% All Labor
Seven 10-hour Days	+ 30% All Labor

Note: NECAnet.org has a research report entitled, *Overtime and Productivity in Electrical Construction*.

Remodel (Old Work)

The only way you can know what adjustments to apply for remodel work, with any degree of accuracy, is to track the labor of every

Understanding Electrical Estimating | Mike Holt Enterprises

remodel job you do and compare the actual hours against the labor unit for future reference.

Once you have some experience and job history, you will be better prepared to adjust the labor for future projects. But doubling the labor unit for fishing and cutting in boxes is not a bad place to start.

Repetition Factor

When you perform the same function over and over again, you complete the task a little faster than the previous time. This will significantly improve your labor productivity.

Consider the following labor adjustments if you have any repetitive work:

Repetitive Labor-Unit Adjustments	
1 to 2 Repeats	0%
3 to 5 Repeats	- 15%
6 to 10 Repeats	- 25%
11 to 15 Repeats	- 35%

Restrictive Working Conditions

Sometimes, due to an accelerated schedule, you will have multiple trades working together in the same room or space (stacking). This forces the trades to work around each other, often resulting in conflict and decreased labor productivity which will increase the number of labor hours required to complete the same work and result in a higher labor unit.

Note: The NECA research report, *Factors Affecting Labor Productivity of Electrical Contractors*, has a section about the stacking of trades.

Schedule

The construction schedule must be taken into consideration when you prepare the estimate. Labor units in all manuals are based on the fact that the job will be properly staffed with sufficient qualified persons, who are properly supervised on a project of normal duration, and using proper tools.

Understanding Electrical Estimating | MikeHolt.com

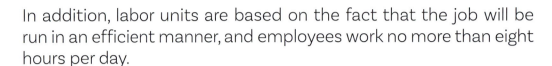

In addition, labor units are based on the fact that the job will be run in an efficient manner, and employees work no more than eight hours per day.

When the project follows an inefficient project progress schedule (accelerated or extended), or the project progress schedule is substantially revised after the project begins, there is a loss of productivity. The magnitude of the productivity loss is related to the circumstances of the project involved, but there is almost always an impact.

Extended-duration jobs resulting from delays due to factors such as weather or poor job management can cause a reduction in labor productivity and an increase in careless mistakes.

Note: NECAnet.org has a research report entitled, *Normal Project Duration.*

Accelerated Schedule

A job that is projected to run on an accelerated schedule requires the electrical contractor to have more manpower on-site than would be typical. This applies not only to the electrical contractor, but also to the other trades. This can result in the contractor needing to hire temporary staff that might not be as well-trained or motivated to produce as the permanent staff.

An accelerated production schedule can cause havoc in scheduling material and tools to be on-site when needed. The impact on labor productivity must be taken into consideration when too many workers are in the same area at the same time. Do not forget to consider the negative effects of increased supervision pressure, or the possible poor productivity of temporary staff.

There is no specific labor adjustment factor for an accelerated schedule, but you should consider its effect on your labor productivity.

Note: NECAnet.org has a research report entitled, *Project Peak Workforce Report.*

Accelerated Schedule Example: What is the crew size for a six-week project that has estimated labor of 1,200 hours?

Crew Size = Total Hours/Number of Weeks/40 hours per week

Crew Size = 1,200 hours/six weeks/40 hours

Crew Size = Five electricians

If you accelerate the schedule to three weeks, you will need twice as many electricians, and your labor productivity will likely decrease, resulting in an increase in labor cost for the job. You may also have to include overtime to meet the compressed scheduling.

Shift Work

When scheduling shift work, take into consideration the lifestyles of your employees. Generally, single employees without parental responsibility prefer to work the second shift (3 p.m. to 11 p.m.), whereas married employees, given the choice between second or third shifts, prefer the third shift (11 p.m. to 7 a.m.). But check with each employee and see what they prefer and, where possible, try to accommodate them.

Shift Work Labor Adjustments			
	Overall	Single	Married
Second Shift	20 to 25%	15 to 20%	25 to 30%
Third Shift	15 to 20%	20 to 25%	15 to 20%

Teamwork

If the general contractor does not coordinate effectively, that deficiency is going to cause everyone problems and probably cost you money.

Understanding Electrical Estimating | MikeHolt.com

When there is tension between the various trades, you can expect problems and a reduction in labor productivity. When possible, try to stimulate and encourage positive teamwork habits between the trades.

Successful electrical contractors provide an incentive plan or reward system to encourage field labor to complete the project within the labor budget. The incentive plan can be paid time off, or perhaps a bonus, based on the number of hours saved compared to the budgeted hours.

Note: NECAnet.org has a research report entitled, *Field Incentive Systems for Electrical Construction.*

Weather/Temperature

Labor units are based on environmental (weather) conditions, which do not reduce labor productivity. Optimum labor efficiency is achieved when the working temperature is between 35°F and 80°F, with a relative humidity below 50 percent.

Studies have shown that extreme temperatures cause workers to concentrate on their discomfort, rather than on the job to be performed. This results in an increase in accidents, deterioration in workmanship, and lower labor productivity.

Cold. Extremely cold conditions cause a significant reduction in labor productivity because of the need for frequent warm-up breaks. Working in extremely cold environments is very uncomfortable and it often leads to head colds or a feeling of being run-down.

Heat. Elevated temperatures cause a decrease in labor productivity due to the time required to wipe body perspiration from one's face, hands, and from work surfaces, making it difficult to handle material, equipment, and tools.

When the temperature is elevated, electricians become fatigued, belligerent, and irritable (let's not go there). They also suffer from diminished powers of concentration under these conditions.

Note: NECAnet.org has a report available entitled, *The Effect of Temperature on Productivity.*

Understanding Electrical Estimating | Mike Holt Enterprises

Are You for Real?

You might be wondering, "If I adjust my labor units to account for these variable factors, how will I ever get a job?"

Let's get real, if you choose not to apply any of these labor-unit adjustments for fear that your price will be too high, and you get the job, you really will be in trouble. Better to not get a job that is priced correctly, than to get a job and just break even—or worse yet, lose money.

Final Thoughts

Your estimating journey has taken you through five chapters so far. You have reviewed what estimating is in Chapter 1, what makes a good estimator in Chapter 2, the estimating process in Chapter 3, the takeoff process in Chapter 4 and now you have the information you need to determine labor costs including:

- What a labor unit is
- What is included in a labor unit
- What is *not* included in a labor unit
- How variables can affect labor-unit calculations

Perhaps the most important thing to understand from this chapter is that you will never find a "one size fits all" set of labor-unit data so make sure you choose a good base set of labor units then use historical data to adjust them to match your company's performance. Next up, we will discuss unit prices and exactly when and where they can effectively be used.

Understanding Electrical Estimating | MikeHolt.com

Use the information you learned in this chapter to answer the following questions.

Chapter 5—Review Questions

5.1 Introduction

1. When you do an electrical estimate, major cost components of the job you will need to determine include _____ and labor.

    (a)   taxes
    (b)   material/equipment
    (c)   insurance
    (d)   special tools

5.2 Basis of a Labor Unit

2. A(An) _____ represents the approximate amount of time required to install an electrical product, component, or piece of equipment.

    (a)   man-hour
    (b)   work-hour
    (c)   labor unit
    (d)   installation unit

3. Labor units are based on the assumption that a skilled electrician is completing the task under a "specific" set of installation conditions, as well as _____.

    (a)   electrician skill and experience
    (b)   adequate supervision
    (c)   appropriate tools
    (d)   all of these

4. Some typical project considerations that should be used for the purposes of estimating using standard labor units include up to three floors and 20,000 to ____ per floor.

   (a) 25,000 sq ft.
   (b) 30,000 sq ft.
   (c) 50,000 sq ft.
   (d) 100,000 sq ft.

5. Typical site considerations to be used for the purposes of estimating using labor unit include that ____ equipment is supplied by others.

   (a) high-reach
   (b) lift
   (c) excavation
   (d) all of these

5.3 Expressing Labor Units

6. Labor hours are expressed in decimal form so that the hours can be added in a manner similar to dollars and cents, rather than having to ____.

   (a) use a calculator
   (b) add hours and minutes individually
   (c) rely on a spreadsheet
   (d) use computer software

7. Work experience is important when calculating labor units because it allows you to foresee the pitfalls of particular types of jobs that could impact ____.

   (a) the outcome
   (b) your liability
   (c) the efficiency of your employees
   (d) customer satisfaction

Understanding Electrical Estimating | MikeHolt.com

8. Factors, such as amount of supervision required, availability of qualified employees, job layout, handling of tools and material, nonproductive time, and job conditions, all influence ____.

   (a) the outcome of a job
   (b) your liability on a job
   (c) the efficiency of employees on a job
   (d) customer satisfaction

5.4 Components of a Labor Unit

9. A labor unit has ____ major components.

   (a) 3
   (b) 4
   (c) 5
   (d) 6

10. The actual installation time only represents about ____ of the labor unit.

    (a) 10 percent
    (b) 12.5 percent
    (c) 25 percent
    (d) 50 percent

11. The layout of the work represents ____ of the labor unit.

    (a) 15 percent
    (b) 12.5 percent
    (c) 25 percent
    (d) 50 percent

12. Material handling and cleanup represents ____ of the labor unit.

    (a) 10 percent
    (b) 12.5 percent
    (c) 25 percent
    (d) 50 percent

13. All jobs include nonproductive labor, which should be managed so as not to exceed _____ of the labor unit.

    (a) 5 percent
    (b) 10 percent
    (c) 12.5 percent
    (d) 15 percent

14. Supervision represents 10 percent of the labor unit and can include _____.

    (a) reviewing the drawings and specifications
    (b) ordering material
    (c) progress reports
    (d) all of these

15. The _____ represent(s) 10 percent of the labor unit.

    (a) management
    (b) handling
    (c) layout
    (d) all of these

5.5 Labor-Unit Manuals

16. Purchase a comprehensive labor-unit manual that contains at least _____ labor units.

    (a) 1,000
    (b) 5,000
    (c) 10,000
    (d) 15,000

17. Using of a labor unit manual along with _____, will develop techniques to help you adjust the labor units, so they represent your productivity under specific job conditions

    (a) a computer
    (b) experience and historical data
    (c) a whiteboard
    (d) common sense

Understanding Electrical Estimating | MikeHolt.com

5.6 Adjusting Labor Units

18. Productivity in the installation of electrical equipment is affected by many factors, and the most significant is ____.

    (a)   lead-time
    (b)   material costs
    (c)   overhead
    (d)   project management

19. Be sure your employees are properly trained in advance in all aspects of their job including safety, the proper use of tools, and ____.

    (a)   the IRC
    (b)   the ICC
    (c)   the NEC
    (d)   local building codes

20. A qualified ____ team can make or break a job. Your managers need to follow the estimate, stay on schedule, and coordinate with other trades throughout the job.

    (a)   field
    (b)   management
    (c)   shop
    (d)   labor

5.7 Labor Unit Variables

21. Data from a labor-unit manual must be adjusted to fit the job conditions that you are dealing with. Labor unit variables with significant impact include ____.

    (a)   working height
    (b)   weather conditions
    (c)   travel distance
    (d)   all of these

22. There are many factors that impact a labor unit. Variables with significant impact include ____.

    (a)   building complexity
    (b)   change orders
    (c)   contractor management
    (d)   all of these

23. Labor unit variables resulting from building complexity might include ____.

    (a)   floor conditions
    (b)   hoisting restrictions
    (c)   working heights
    (d)   all of these

24. When considering a project's working height, labor units are based on buildings and projects with up to ____ floors above grade or street level.

    (a)   two
    (b)   three
    (c)   four
    (d)   five

25. Multi-story labor unit adjustments should include adding ____ percent times the height of the single floor level you are working on.

    (a)   one
    (b)   two
    (c)   three
    (d)   four

26. Labor units are based on the effective coordination and management of the project. The effects of poor project management might include ____.

    (a)   an accelerated construction schedule
    (b)   excessive change orders
    (c)   overtime
    (d)   all of these

Understanding Electrical Estimating | MikeHolt.com

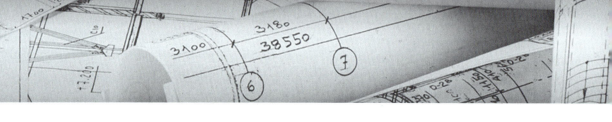

27. Labor unit variables pertaining to jobsite factors might include abnormal conditions such as ____.

    (a) delivery restrictions
    (b) parking restrictions
    (c) storage restrictions
    (d) all of these

28. Out-of-town work will have a significant effect on labor unit adjustments so remember to consider items such as ____.

    (a) local pay scale
    (b) travel time
    (c) lodging
    (d) all of these

29. Other considerations that can have an effect on labor units are ____.

    (a) having qualified personnel
    (b) your attitude and staff motivation
    (c) employee training
    (d) all of these

30. Additional labor unit variables to be considered for adjustments are installations that are more labor intensive such as ____.

    (a) embedded wiring
    (b) exposed wiring
    (c) ladder and scaffold work
    (d) all of these

31. Labor units are based on normal work schedules of 8 daylight hours per day, five days per week, and 40 total hours per week, with a minimum amount of overtime ____.

    (a) one day a week
    (b) once or twice a month
    (c) one weekend a month
    (d) no more than three times in a month

32. There is ____ labor adjustment factor for an accelerated schedule, but you should consider its effect on your labor productivity.

(a) only a minimal
(b) only a one percent
(c) no specific
(d) only a two percent

33. Labor units are based on weather conditions, and optimum labor efficiency is achieved when the working temperature is between ____, with a relative humidity below 50 percent.

(a) 35 and 80 degrees Fahrenheit
(b) 25 and 85 degrees Fahrenheit
(c) 40 and 85 degrees Fahrenheit
(d) 30 and 90 degrees Fahrenheit

Understanding Electrical Estimating | MikeHolt.com

Notes...

2nd Printing

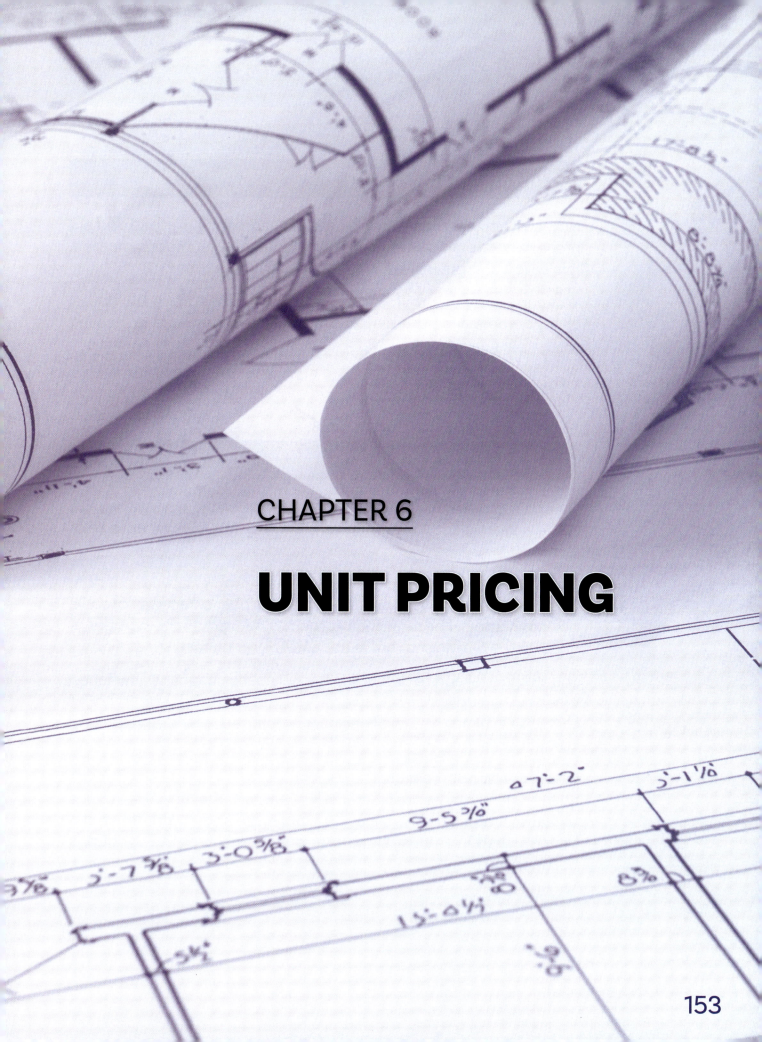

CHAPTER 6

UNIT PRICING

6.1 Introduction

Now that you have learned the detailed estimating method and bid process, we are going to show you an alternative estimating method. It is called unit pricing, and using it will save you time.

You can safely use unit pricing on renovations, office buildouts, change orders, and other simple or small-scope jobs. Here we'll cover:

6.2   **What Is Unit Pricing?**

6.3   **Unit Pricing Applications**

6.2 What Is Unit Pricing?

Unit pricing refers to the practice of developing an average price to install a given electrical component, such as a duplex receptacle or a switch.

This price includes the outlet box, average number of wire connectors, mounting hardware, and the typical number of raceway or cable box connectors. The unit price is then multiplied by the number of units on the drawings to arrive at a total bid price for the installation.

You still do a takeoff to determine the number of luminaries, switches, receptacles, and so forth. However, you just do not separately count the boxes, fittings, and other parts included in the unit pricing components.

Often you do not measure the wiring runs for every opening but use an average length per installed outlet as part of the "unit." Homeruns to panelboards, communications cabinets, and so on, must still be measured in the usual manner due to the extreme variations between each one.

6.3 Unit Pricing Applications

Advantages

Unit pricing is faster and easier than the detailed estimating method described in earlier chapters. Because it takes less time, it costs your company less money to determine the selling price for a job.

Unit pricing is relatively accurate on repetitive jobs in which many identical items of electrical equipment will be installed under the same (or fairly similar) conditions. As a result, unit pricing is much easier to execute on the fly.

Disadvantages

Unit pricing is not suitable for jobs where the assemblies are not identical.

For example, if you have 200 identical fluorescent luminaries to install in a building where the ceiling heights vary from 8 ft to 15 ft in different areas. The unit prices will need to be adjusted to an average luminaire height, or different unit prices will need to be applied for the different ceiling heights, eliminating the main advantage of unit pricing.

It is easier to demonstrate this concept with an example rather than trying to explain it in words. Look at the following table to see how a $72.74 unit price for a single-pole switch is calculated, using the following factors:

- Labor hour adjustment (10%)
- Labor cost ($18 per man-hour)
- Material cost adjustment—(15% waste, theft, miscellaneous)
- Sales Tax (7%)
- Overhead ($18 per man-hour)
- Profit (15% of selling price)

Understanding Electrical Estimating | MikeHolt.com

Unit Cost—Single-Pole Switch

Item #	Item Description	Qty	Cost	Ext Cost	Labor Unit	Ext Hrs	Unit	%
31	Metal Boxes 4 × 4" Regular	1	$47.84	$0.48	18.00	0.18	100	
1711	Rings, 1-Gang	1	$39.00	$0.39	4.50	0.05	100	
315	EMT Set Screw Connectors ½"	2	$9.43	$0.19	2.00	0.04	100	
305	EMT ½"	20	$19.39	$3.88	2.25	0.45	100	
355	EMT Set Screw Couplings ½"	1	$9.70	$0.10	2.00	0.02	100	
415	EMT Straps 1-Hole ½"	3	$3.10	$0.09	2.50	0.08	100	
2091	Switches—15A, 125V, 1-Pole	1	$58.23	$0.58	20.00	0.20	100	
1261	Plates, Plastic 1-Gang Switch	1	$18.88	$0.19	2.50	0.03	100	
2391	Wire—12 THHN, Copper, 600V	50	$73.69	$3.68	4.25	0.21	1,000	
Subtotal				**$9.58**		1.26 hr		
Labor								
Labor Hours with Adjustment				10%				
Labor Cost				$18.00		1.39 hr	$25.02	34.40%
Material								
Material Cost with Adjustment				15%	$11.02			
Sales Tax				7%	$0.77			
Material Cost							$11.79	16.21%
Unit Price Summary								
Prime Cost (Material + Labor)							$36.81	50.60%
Overhead				$18.00			$25.02	34.40%
Break-Even Cost							$61.83	85.00%
Profit 15% (17.65% Markup Multiplier)				17.65%			$10.91	14.83%
Unit Price							**$72.74**	**100.00%**

From the table, you can see that the unit pricing method can be a real time saver. Do not let this lull you into trading time for the accuracy required for more detailed estimating projects.

Final Thoughts

You have now completed Chapter 6 and understand the limited but important role unit pricing can play in the estimating process. Unit pricing is faster and easier than the detailed estimating method. It has pros and cons and isn't the right fit for every situation. But it can be used on service work, small renovations, office buildouts, change orders, and other simple or small-scope jobs with a lot of repetition.

Before we move on to Chapter 7 and learn about Break-Even cost, take a moment to think about Chapters 1-6 and how all these chapters present methods to determine how much it costs to complete a scope of work. In Chapter 7 you will learn to take that information and apply it to your business metrics to determine what the break-even cost is for your specific company to complete the work contained in your estimate.

Use the information you learned in this chapter to answer the following questions.

Chapter 6—Review Questions

6.1 Introduction

1.   You can safely use unit pricing on ____.

   (a)   renovations
   (b)   change orders
   (c)   small scope jobs
   (d)   all of these

6.2 What Is Unit Pricing?

2.   Unit pricing consists of developing a(an) ____ price to install a given electrical component, such as a duplex receptacle or a switch.

   (a)   average
   (b)   profitable
   (c)   above average
   (d)   below average

6.3 Unit Pricing Applications

3.   Unit pricing is ____ on repetitive jobs.

   (a)   not as accurate
   (b)   unreliable
   (c)   relatively accurate
   (d)   inefficient

4. Unit pricing is ____ for jobs where the assemblies are not identical.

(a) acceptable
(b) not suitable
(c) accurate
(d) reliable

5. A unit price should include a ____ labor adjustment.

(a) 2 percent
(b) 5 percent
(c) 10 percent
(d) 12.5 percent

6. A unit price should include a material cost adjustment of ____.

(a) 2 percent
(b) 5 percent
(c) 15 percent
(d) 17.5 percent

7. A unit price should include a profit of ____.

(a) 2 percent
(b) 5 percent
(c) 10 percent
(d) 15 percent

Notes...

2nd Printing

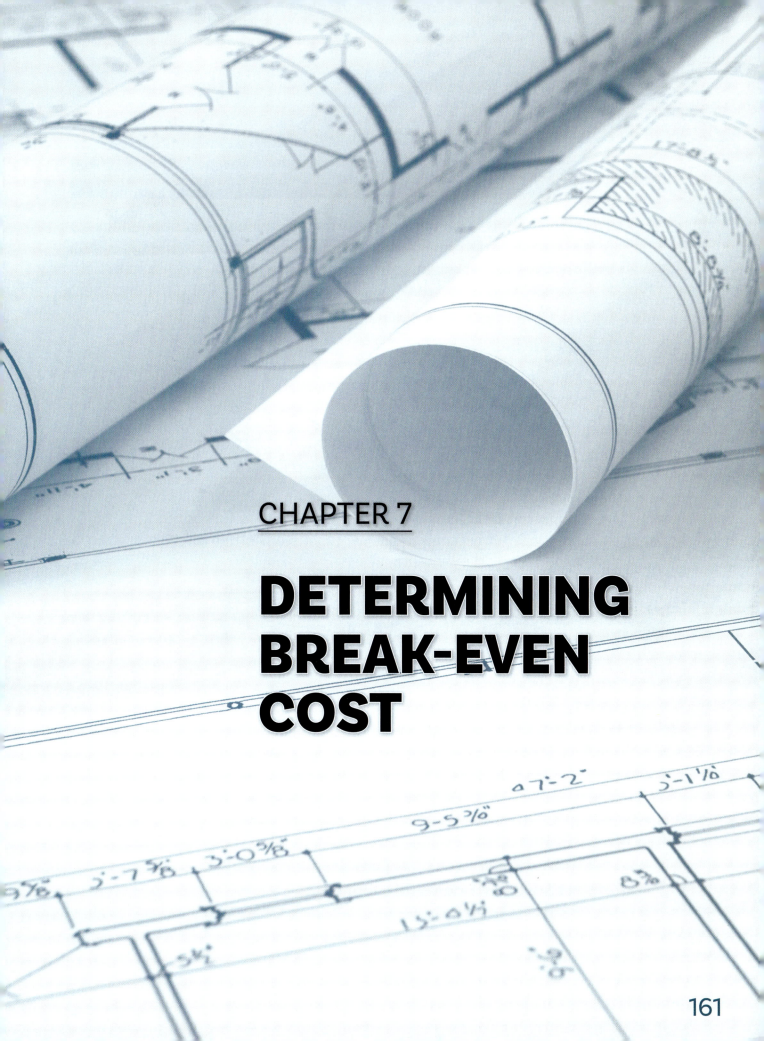

CHAPTER 7

DETERMINING BREAK-EVEN COST

7.1 Introduction

In this chapter, you will learn how to determine the component costs of the job to determine where the break-even point is. This process is not as easy as it might seem, but we will show you a method to help simplify things and make your results consistent and dependable.

Obviously, nobody wants to just break even on a job. So, why calculate the break-even cost?

Think of the break-even cost as a line in the sand that is the point where at the completion of a job, all costs and overhead are covered with neither profit nor loss on the job. Once your bid price covers all of your job costs (the break-even point), every dollar above that is a dollar of profit—but every dollar below it is a dollar of loss.

Throughout the break-even analysis process, you will have to make judgment decisions on intangibles, such as job conditions, labor productivity, material requirements, waste, theft, small tools, direct-job expenses, and overhead.

Remember, making a judgment decision does not mean tossing a coin. Making a sound judgment decision requires obtaining and evaluating all available relevant information, and then logically analyzing your options.

Once you understand the methodology for determining the break-even point, you will be able to avoid the related pitfalls that have put many electrical contractors out of business.

The key to this, however, is your determination to stick to that method and work past the frustration that can arise during this process. Do that, and you are more likely to consistently have an accurate break-even analysis. The following considerations are covered in this chapter:

7.2   **Break-Even Cost Summary Worksheet**

7.3   **Labor Hours and Labor Cost**

7.4   **Material Cost**

7.5   **Direct-Job Expenses**

7.6   Estimated Prime Cost

7.7   Overhead

7.8   Break-Even Cost Review

7.2 Break-Even Cost Summary Worksheet

Summarizing the estimate to determine your break-even cost can be overwhelming. One mistake at this point can be costly in terms of losing a job or worse yet, securing a job at a loss!

This is the part of the estimating process that requires you to make the judgment calls on job conditions, labor productivity, miscellaneous material requirements, waste, theft, small tools, direct-job expenses, and overhead.

The first step in this process is to transfer the totals for labor hours and material costs to a summary worksheet. This worksheet organizes these cost factors so that there is less likelihood of a mistake.

The summary worksheet has seven major sections, and they include:

- Step 1—Labor Hours
- Step 2—Labor Cost
- Step 3—Material Cost
- Step 4—Direct Job Cost
- Step 5—Prime Cost
- Step 6—Overhead
- Step 7—Break-Even Cost

Understanding Electrical Estimating | MikeHolt.com

Summary Worksheet		
Labor Cost Summary		
Step 1	Labor Hours	81.94
	Adjusted Labor Hours	4.09
	Additional Labor Hours	23.74
	Total Adjusted Labor Hours	109.77
Step 2	Labor Cost @$18.00 per hour	$1,975.86
Material Cost Summary		
Step 3	Material Cost (Price Sheet)	$1,804.37
	Miscellaneous Material @ 10%	$ 180.44
	Small Tools @ 3%	$ 54.13
	Waste and Theft @ 5%	$ 90.22
	Taxable Material	$2,129.16
	Sales tax @ 7%	$ 149.04
	Total Material Cost	$2,278.20
Break-Even Cost		
Step 4	Direct Job Costs	$ 550.00
Step 5	Prime Costs (Steps 1,2,3, and 4)	$4,804.06
Step 6	Overhead	$1,975.86
Step 7	Break-Even	$6,779.92

7.3 Labor Hours and Labor Cost

Determining your break-even labor cost requires you to adjust your labor hours for working conditions based on a percentage for specific conditions. You obtain the adjusted labor hour total by multiplying the total hours and the adjustment percentage.

With experience and historical data, adjusting labor hours for job conditions can be quite accurate. Once you have filled out and totaled the labor unit adjustment worksheet enter the adjusted number on the summary worksheet.bor unit adjustment worksheet enter the adjusted number on the summary worksheet.

Labor-Unit Adjustments		
Estimated Labor Hours		**81.94**
Building Conditions	0%	0
Change Orders	0%	0.00
Embedded and Exposed Wiring	0%	0.00
Construction Schedule	0%	0.00
Job Location	0%	0.00
Labor Skill	0%	0.00
Ladder and Scaffold Work	10%	8.19
Management	0%	0.00
Material	0%	0.00
Remodel (Old Work)	0%	0.00
Repetitive Factor	0%	0.00
Restrictive Working Conditions	0%	0.00
Shift Work	0%	0.00
Teamwork	-5%	-4.10
Temperature	0%	0.00
Labor-Unit Adjustment Hours		4.09
Total Labor Hours Including Labor-Unit Adjustments		86.03

Additional Labor

After you have adjusted the total labor-unit hours, you must consider all necessary additional labor requirements for the job. Be aware that these conditions are not adjustments of the labor unit for job conditions, but additional labor that might be required, such as shown in the following table:

Understanding Electrical Estimating | MikeHolt.com

Additional Labor			
Description	Hr	%	Hrs
Total Labor Hours Including Labor-Unit Adjustments			**86.03**
As-Built Drawings			0.00
Demolition	8		8.00
Environmentally Hazardous Material Disposal			0.00
Excavation, Trenching, and Backfill			0.00
Job Location			0.00
Jobsite Meetings	2		2.00
Match-Up of Existing Equipment			0.00
Miscellaneous Material Items		8%	6.88
Mobilization and Demobilization	4		4.00
Nonproductive Labor			0.00
Plans and Specifications			0.00
Power			0.00
Public Safety			0.00
Security			0.00
Service and Warranty	2		2.00
Site Conditions			0.00
Subcontract Supervision			0.00
Training		1%	0.86
Additional Labor Hours			**23.74**
Total Labor Hours Including Additional Labor			**109.77**

As-Built Drawings

As-built drawings are intended to show, in accurate detail, the location of feeders, branch circuits, and the size of the electrical equipment. These are typically produced by the original architect or engineer since many jobs require these to be done in an electronic form, by using AutoCAD or a .pdf file.

If this responsibility happens to fall on you as required by the contract and specifications, be sure to include the labor to create and maintain as-built drawings. Some contractors may have the capability to do this in-house, whereas others will need to hire someone to do them.

Demolition

Some jobs require the removal of the existing electrical wiring and equipment before you begin adding anything new. The labor for demolition must be considered, and this is one of those times where these costs might be just an educated guess until you can rely on historical data.

With experience you will get a feel as to what might be reasonable and profitable.

Be sure to verify whether the demolition will be to "disconnect and make safe" for others to do the actual removals, or if you will need to perform both the disconnecting and removal operations.

Environmentally Hazardous Material

Be sure the bid includes the labor and any special considerations required to handle environmentally hazardous material.

This includes preparation, packaging, shipping, and the proper disposal of ballasts, electric-discharge lamps, radioactive exit signs, personal protective gear, and so on. With all that may be involved, it's probably a good idea to subcontract this work to a company that specializes in hazardous material removal.

Excavation, Trenching, and Backfill

There are places in the country where you cannot plant a bush without a pick. Conversely, if you try to dig a trench in sugar sand on the beach, the more you dig the wider the trench gets—but it does not get any deeper.

Understanding Electrical Estimating | MikeHolt.com

Poor soil conditions can turn what was anticipated to be a simple job into a major project. It is often more cost-effective to subcontract this type of work rather than take the entire responsibility of accidentally cutting fiber optic cable, telephone wires, underground high-voltage utility lines, sprinkler and water pipes, or a gas main.

Word of Caution: Before beginning any kind of excavation, make certain that you are aware of any existing underground utilities and their location(s) to ensure that they are avoided. These are typically indicated on the site plan, but if not, it is your responsibility to obtain this information "before you dig." There may be substantial fines and penalties imposed for any damages created if you don't!

Job Location

If the job is not located near your shop, you need to add travel time. Also consider that it will be more difficult to manage the job and to get the material there when needed.

The following example should help you understand how to determine travel time.

Travel Time Example: What is the total travel time required for a 212-hour job that has three workers, assuming travel time of 1 hour per worker per day?

(a) 5.25 hours   (b) 8.75 hours   (c) 10 hours   (d) 30 hours

Answer: (d) 30 hours

Job Days = Total Job Hours/Hours Worked per Day
Job Days = 212 hours/21 hours/day (3 workers at 7 hours/day)
Job Days = 10 travel days

Travel Time = 1 hour/day per worker x 3 workers x 10 days
Travel time = 30 hours

Job Meetings

Do not forget to add labor for jobsite safety meetings and other planned meetings of jobsite staff. You might be required to attend meetings, even before your phase of the job begins, so be sure to check the plans and specifications carefully.

Also, try to anticipate a reasonable number of trades meetings which help in overall job production scheduling, and prevent the different trades from working on top of each other. These meetings are usually attended by either yourself, your lead or job foreman.

Match-Up of Existing Equipment

Maybe you have a situation where you are required to match existing equipment, colors, or luminaries. This can become very time consuming and costly, so be sure to account for this expense.

Miscellaneous Material Items

It is impractical to try to determine the labor for every material item required for a job. Add eight percent to the total estimated labor hours for miscellaneous material items not counted or measured when using the manual estimating method.

There is typically no need to make any labor-hour adjustment for miscellaneous material items in a computer-assisted estimate because the software accounts for all material required to complete the job.

Mobilization and Demobilization

Do not forget to include the labor required to set up and close down the job, such as preparing the job trailer to be moved.

Understanding Electrical Estimating | MikeHolt.com

Nonproductive Labor

Labor units include a prorated amount of the normal nonproductive labor experienced on a typical project. On some projects the nonproductive labor is greater than the normal amount, and the estimated labor for the installation of the electrical systems must be increased accordingly.

For example, the owner or general contractor may allow or require all construction crafts to take coffee breaks at a specific time and a specific duration. The evaluation and determination of the magnitude of abnormal productivity is extremely difficult because there are no standard percentages, mathematical formulas, or guidelines that can be used.

The evaluation of the cause and effect of abnormal nonproductive situations can only be determined by the judgment of an experienced person. In estimating the project labor requirements, the electrical contractor must evaluate all the known and anticipated project conditions that will affect the labor productivity. After this, you can adjust the estimated labor man-hours accordingly.

Breaks

When you are on a job for a while, your employees get to know other trade workers. As a result, breaks tend to become longer and more frequent if they do not have proper supervision.

Distracting Job Conditions

Is this job going to be directly on a beach, marina, or other areas where the workers will be distracted? If that's the case, you'll need to increase the labor requirements by some factor to account for distractions during work hours.

If you bid on a job at a theme park or beach, you should increase the labor requirements for distractions!

Inspection Tours

Inspection tours are a fact of life, and the larger the job, the more frequent and longer the tours. Sometimes projects have multiple inspectors for the different systems—often by different inspection agencies. Do not forget about these!

Plans and Specifications

If adequate drawings and specifications are not provided, add a factor to account for anticipated nonproductive time spent to figure out what is required. Labor units assume that you have clear and conflict-free drawings and specifications. If this is not the case, inform the general contractor or the owner that your bid includes additional labor as a contingency.

Power

Labor to ensure that temporary, standby, or emergency power is available must be included in the bid if required. Remember to take any need for maintenance into consideration too.

Public Safety

Public safety is a factor—especially when doing work for city, county, state, or federal governmental agencies. Are you required to install traffic cones, barricades, or security gates? Will you be required to have flaggers, or possibly stand-by personnel?

Be sure to read the specifications closely and plan your estimate accordingly to account for labor as well as the cost for safety products.

Always verify what job specific safety meetings and requirements are included in your scope of work. Safety requirements, such as required breaks or safety meetings, that were not included in the estimate could have a devastating impact on your labor budget.

Understanding Electrical Estimating | MikeHolt.com

Security

When working in some government or private facilities, you are required to follow specific procedures to receive clearance to enter the premises. Some facilities require that security be notified well in advance of persons desiring entry into the premises, and they have to wait for someone to escort them while in the facility.

Include monies for badges and drug testing because your personnel might also have to have drug testing done or attend site-specific orientation meetings or courses.

Service and Warranty

No job is installed perfectly, so add some labor to cover service and warranty work.

Site Conditions

Because of traffic conditions, projects in the downtown areas of large cities can cause significant lost time. Traffic conditions and narrow streets make it difficult to unload material and equipment. Inadequate parking and storage space are also potential problems. Parking costs in large cities like Chicago can be very expensive, in the range of $25 to $50 per day.

Subcontract Supervision

Do not forget to include the labor required for your electricians to supervise and direct subcontractors.

Training

Do you pay your electricians to attend a training and certification program? Include the cost of regular safety training and any required personal protective equipment (PPE) that you provide. It will be wise to add one percent to cover labor training.

Labor-Cost Example

The estimated labor cost for a job is determined by multiplying the total adjusted labor man-hours by the labor rate per man-hour.

 Labor Cost Example: The total adjusted estimated labor is 109.77 hours and the labor rate per man-hour is $18.00.

Estimated Labor Cost = Total Adjusted Estimated Labor Hours × Labor Rate per Man-Hour

Estimated Labor Cost = 109.77 hours × $18.00

Estimated Labor Cost = $1,975.86

Summary Worksheet		
Labor Cost Summary		
Step 1	Labor Hours	81.94
	Adjusted Labor Hours	4.09
	Additional Labor Hours	23.74
	Total Adjusted Labor Hours	109.77
Step 2	Labor Cost @$18.00 per hour	**$1,975.86**

Labor Rate per Hour

The labor rate per labor hour can be determined by one of two labor rates:

- Shop Average
- Job Average

The labor rate per man-hour is significantly different in different parts of the country. In some areas, a journeyman electrician is paid less than $20 per hour, and in other areas, the rate is over $50 per hour.

Understanding Electrical Estimating | MikeHolt.com

Shop Average

The shop average labor rate per man-hour is determined by dividing the total field labor cost over a given period of time by the total number of field man-hours over the same period of time.

When using shop average for labor rate per man-hour, it might be too low for jobs that require greater skill (such as control wiring), or too high for simple jobs that require less skill (such as residential wiring).

Shop Average Labor Rate Calculation Example			
Month	Labor Cost	Hours	Rate/Hr
April	$24,000	1,166	$20.58
May	$30,000	1,666	$18.01
June	$36,000	2,167	$16.61
July	$24,000	1,250	$19.20
August	$30,000	1,584	$18.94
September	$36,000	2,167	$16.61
Six Months	$180,000	10,000	$18.00

Job Average

Another approach in determining the labor rate per man-hour is to use the anticipated job average labor rate per man-hour.

This method requires you to consider how you plan on manning the job, such as who will be there, and what the skill level and wage rate are appropriate.

For "prevailing wage" jobs, be sure to use the rate required in the specifications.

Review the following example:

Job Average Labor Rate Calculation Example			
Crew	Rate	# of Persons	Extension
Foreman	$25.00	1	$25.00
Journeyman	$20.00	1	$20.00
Apprentice	$15.00	3	$45.00
Total		5	$90.00
Weighted Rate-Per-Hour			**$18.00**

Labor Burden Costs

In addition to the cost of labor, there are other costs associated with labor that must be taken into consideration. These include employer-paid Social Security and Medicare taxes, Workers' Compensation insurance, as well as employee benefits. These costs are identified as labor burden costs. Here are three Labor burden costs that must be considered:

- Payroll Taxes
- Workers' Compensation
- Employee Benefits

Payroll Taxes

The following are some of the common federal and state taxes. We can round this off to about 10 percent.

- Social Security FICA tax rate = 6.2 percent
- Social Security wage limit = $168,600*
- Federal unemployment tax (FUTA) = 6 percent of the first $7,000 of wages*
- Medicare contribution = 1.45 percent of the total wages*
- State unemployment tax can be as much as 12 percent, so verify your local rate.

*Make sure to verify these numbers with your accountant before including them in a bid.

Understanding Electrical Estimating | MikeHolt.com

Workers' Compensation

The percentage is based on total wages paid and varies from state to state and from contractor to contractor. It is based on the contractor's number of years in business in the state and any claims-related experience.

Workers' Compensation, unlike payroll taxes, is applied to total wages, and the cost should be between 7 and 15 percent of the total payroll.

Employee Benefits

Employee benefits might include life, accident and health insurance plans, pension plans, civic and personal leave, and severance, vacation, and holiday pay. A reasonable number is about 25 percent, at a minimum.

Labor burden expenses are generally listed in the income statement under overhead. When this occurs, labor burden will be applied to the estimate when overhead is applied. We will assume that is the case for the purpose of this textbook.

7.4 Material Cost

After you transfer the material cost from your price/labor worksheets to your estimate summary worksheet, the next step is to calculate total material cost. As part of this process, you will account for the following line items:

- Lighting Fixtures
- Miscellaneous Material
- Switchgear Quotes
- Tools
- Waste and Theft (Shrinkage)
- Sales Tax
- Summary Worksheet

Lighting Fixtures

In an attempt to maintain high-profit margins, lighting suppliers often withhold prices until the last moment, so their competitors will not have a chance to undercut them.

You need to have your estimate summary worksheet completed ahead of time. If the quoted items have not been inserted, then a reasonable "guess" must be noted instead. This will avoid an omission of high-value materials.

This way, when the last-minute quote prices arrive, you can determine the bid price.

Be sure to review the quote when it arrives to ensure substitutions were not made. If they were, you may need to talk to the supplier to ensure you will not have to bear an additional cost if the substitutions are not acceptable.

Miscellaneous Material

It is impractical to try to determine every material item required for a job, like mounting screws, pulling compound, paper towels, safety gear, wire connectors, tape, and so on.

You can either try to count them in your takeoff or add a percentage to the total cost of material as an adjustment. I suggest you add 10 percent of the material cost as a factor when you are doing the estimate manually, or two to three percent adjustment for computer-assisted takeoff.

Switchgear Quotes

Much like lighting suppliers, switchgear suppliers may withhold pricing in an attempt to maintain high-profit margins.

Make sure to have your estimate summary worksheet completed ahead of time and insert a reasonable "guess" with a note until the actual price is received. This will reduce the chance that you omit a high value materials quote.

Understanding Electrical Estimating | MikeHolt.com

Tools

Costs for ladders, cords, cordless drills, screw guns, drill bits, hacksaw blades, and countless other small tools must be included in the estimate. A factor of three percent of the total material cost is considered an acceptable value for small tools.

Waste and Theft (Shrinkage)

Shrinkage is a term often used to describe the effects of waste and theft of material on the jobsite. For an efficiently managed job, five percent is reasonable, but you will not know until you have historical data.

Sales Tax

Sales tax procedures vary from state to state, county to county, and also from city to city. Be sure you are familiar with the sales tax rules in the area where the job is located.

Material Cost Totals—Sales Tax		
Description	%	Cost
Estimated Material Cost		$1,804.37
Lighting Fixture Quote		$0.00
Miscellaneous Material	10%	$180.44
Small Tools	3%	$54.13
Switch Gear Quote		$0.00
Waste and Theft	5%	$90.22
Taxable Material		$2,129.16
Sales Tax	7%	$149.04
Total Material Cost		$2,278.20

2nd Printing

Word of Caution: Do not forget to include freight and shipping costs (which are not taxable).

Summary Worksheet

At this point, you are ready to transfer the total material cost totals to the summary worksheet.

Summary Worksheet		
Labor Cost Summary		
Step 1	Labor Hours	81.94
	Adjusted Labor Hours	4.09
	Additional Labor Hours	23.74
	Total Adjusted Labor Hours	109.77
Step 2	Labor Cost @$18.00 per hour	$1,975.86
Material Cost Summary		
Step 3	Material Cost (Price Sheet)	$1,804.37
	Miscellaneous Material @ 10%	$ 180.44
	Small Tools @ 3%	$ 54.13
	Waste and Theft @ 5%	$ 90.22
	Taxable Material	$2,129.16
	Sales tax @ 7%	$ 149.04
	Total Material Cost	$2,278.20
Break-Even Cost		
Step 4	Direct Job Costs	$ 550.00
Step 5	Prime Costs (A, B, C, and D)	$4,804.06
Step 6	Overhead	$1,975.86
Step 7	Break-Even	$6,779.92

Understanding Electrical Estimating | MikeHolt.com

7.5 Direct-Job Expenses

The next step in determining the break-even cost is to account for direct-job expenses. These are often not shown on the drawings but are probably indicated in the contract or specifications. Fill in the Direct-Job Expenses Worksheet and transfer the total to the Summary Worksheet.

Direct-Job Expenses	
Allowance and Contingencies	$0.00
Business and Occupational Fees	$50.00
Coordination Drawings	$0.00
Engineering/Working Drawings	$0.00
Equipment/Rental	$200.00
Job Insurance/Bond	$0.00
OSHA Compliance (Safety Equipment)	$0.00
Out-of-Town Expenses	$0.00
Parking Fees	$0.00
Permits and Inspection Fees	$300.00
Public Safety	$0.00
Recycling Fees	$0.00
Storage	$0.00
Temporary Power	$0.00
Testing and Certification Fees	$0.00
Trash Disposal	$0.00
Utility Charges and Fees	$0.00
Total Direct-Job Expenses	**$550.00**

Allowances and Contingencies. If the specifications require an allowance to cover the cost of certain items, be sure your bid includes this. You might also want to consider a contingency clause to protect yourself against dramatic cost increases in steel conduit and copper wire prices.

Business and Occupational Fees. If you need to purchase a business license or pay an occupational fee for the job, be sure your estimate includes this expense.

Coordination Drawings. It is becoming commonplace for the MEP (Mechanical, Electrical, and Plumbing) trades to complete coordination drawings prior to the actual installation. The drawings account for the clashes and collisions in the limited-ceiling areas and mechanical rooms for these infrastructure installations.

Be certain to account for CAD personnel, coordination meeting time, and drawing reprographics in your estimate.

Engineering/Working Drawings. If you intend to make changes to the job's design, particularly for value-engineered jobs (an alternate means of accomplishing the same end result), you will need to submit revised drawings. Do *not* forget to include architectural or engineering costs in your estimate.

Equipment/Rental. Remember to include the cost for equipment, trailers, computers, fax and copy machines, radios and cell phones, office personnel, vehicles, and any other such job-related expenses.

Job Insurance/Bond. Be careful, the specifications might require you to secure insurance and/or performance bonding. Do not miss this!

OSHA Compliance. Be sure to include OSHA-related products such as safety rails, straps, personal protective equipment (PPE), and ladder tie-downs.

Out-of-Town Expenses. When bidding a job outside your local area, consider travel expenses, tolls, gas, lodging, meals, internet access, and long-distance telephone calls or cell phones.

Parking Fees. Parking fees for jobs in major cities can be very expensive!

Understanding Electrical Estimating | MikeHolt.com

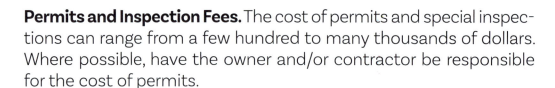

Permits and Inspection Fees. The cost of permits and special inspections can range from a few hundred to many thousands of dollars. Where possible, have the owner and/or contractor be responsible for the cost of permits.

Public Safety. Public safety is a factor, especially when doing work for city, county, state, or federal governmental agencies. Are you required to purchase or rent safety cones, barricades, or security gates? What about security personnel?

Recycling Fees. Federal and state laws often require the proper disposal of environmentally hazardous products. Watch out for this when disposing of existing electrical products that might contain hazardous chemicals within the product.

Storage. Storage space on the jobsite is often a must, so be sure to include this cost (containers/trailers) in the estimate.

> **Word of Caution:** If the job turns bad, you might not be permitted back on the jobsite to remove your trailer, material, tools, or equipment. If things appear to be going sour, get your trailer and equipment off the job to a safe location as quickly as possible.

> **Case Study No. 1:** I know of a few cases where the owners did not pay the electrical contractors and prevented them from entering the premises to retrieve their material, equipment, and tools. By the time the contractors secured a court order requiring the owner to give access, their equipment and tools were long gone—with the owner claiming no knowledge of their whereabouts!

Temporary Power. When estimating temporary power, be sure you are clear in your proposal as to what you intend to provide.

Do not agree to vague phrases in the contract such as, "Provide temporary power as needed." Be specific in your proposal and indicate the size and voltage of the service, number of poles, lights, receptacles, switches, and any other item that might be required.

If your bid does not include maintenance and repairs, or utility connection charges, be sure to document it in your proposal. Sometimes it is more practical to do a takeoff of the temporary power during the takeoff phase of the estimate.

Case Study No. 2: The contract specified that the electrical contractor would supply all temporary power. He failed to visit the jobsite and assumed a basic temporary pole in the estimate. But later (after winning the bid) he found out that no electric utility power was available within two miles of the job. He was required to supply generators for one year, including the cost of fuel and maintenance.

Testing and Certification Fees. Do the job specifications require that electrical systems be tested and/or certified in some manner, like meggering the wiring or ground resistance validation?

Trash Disposal. Who covers the cost of trash that has to be removed from the site? If it is thrown in the dumpster, will you be charged a portion of the overall cost by the general contractor? Make sure your contract is clear on this subject.

Utility Charges and Fees. Who is responsible for paying the electric utility service deposit and monthly electric charge?

Understanding Electrical Estimating | MikeHolt.com

7.6 Estimated Prime Cost

Estimated Prime Cost is a term used to identify the subtotaled cost of labor, material, and direct costs. Overhead is to be applied to this entire number. The term allows us to clearly identify the cost number that we will add overhead cost to.

Various electrical estimating software programs may use terms such as Raw Costs, Job Subtotal, or simply Subtotal. Whatever term is used, the function of that term remains the same.

Calculating your estimated prime cost is just the simple matter of adding up the labor, material, and direct job costs.

Estimated Prime Cost		
Labor Cost (Hrs × Rate)	$18.00	$1,975.86
Labor Burden (Included When Overhead is Applied)		$0.00
Material Cost		$2,278.20
Direct Job Cost		$550.00
Prime Cost		**$4,804.06**

7.7 Overhead

The cost related to the operation and management of the company, such as rent, insurance, vehicles, administrative salaries, professional fees, and so on, is known as overhead. This amount is usually obtained from your income statement or your accountant.

Smaller-Sized Contractor Income Statement Year Ending December 31		
Sales	$250,000	100% of Sales
Direct Job Cost		
Labor (4,000 Hrs)	$80,000	
Material	$70,000	
Total Direct Cost (Prime Cost)	$150,000	60% of Sales
Gross Profit	$100,000	40% of Sales
Overhead Expenses (Administrative Cost)		
Salaries and Commissions	$15,000	
Advertising	$5,000	
Auto and Gas	$10,000	
Benefits	$20,000	
Interest	$1,000	
Insurance—Auto, General, Workman's Comp.	$5,000	
Miscellaneous Expense	$3,000	
Payroll Taxes	$8,000	
Rent	$5,000	
Utilities/Phone	$3,000	
Total Administrative Expenses (50% of Prime)	$75,000	30% of Sales
Net Profit Before Taxes (16.67% of Prime)	$25,000	10% of Sales

As your annual business volume and revenue increase, the cost of overhead per labor hour decreases because it's split across more jobs. As a result, smaller jobs and/or smaller-sized contractors have a higher ratio of overhead cost to labor as compared to larger jobs or larger size contractors. This requires them to be very efficient to maximize profit.

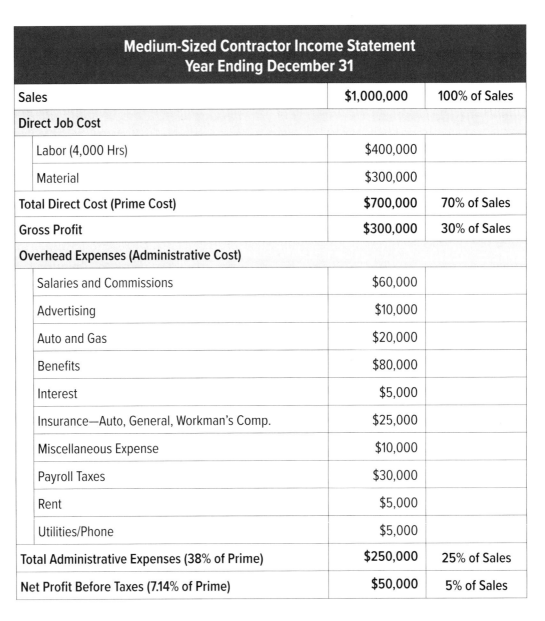

Medium-Sized Contractor Income Statement Year Ending December 31		
Sales	$1,000,000	100% of Sales
Direct Job Cost		
Labor (4,000 Hrs)	$400,000	
Material	$300,000	
Total Direct Cost (Prime Cost)	$700,000	70% of Sales
Gross Profit	$300,000	30% of Sales
Overhead Expenses (Administrative Cost)		
Salaries and Commissions	$60,000	
Advertising	$10,000	
Auto and Gas	$20,000	
Benefits	$80,000	
Interest	$5,000	
Insurance—Auto, General, Workman's Comp.	$25,000	
Miscellaneous Expense	$10,000	
Payroll Taxes	$30,000	
Rent	$5,000	
Utilities/Phone	$5,000	
Total Administrative Expenses (38% of Prime)	$250,000	25% of Sales
Net Profit Before Taxes (7.14% of Prime)	$50,000	5% of Sales

While the overhead calculation is beyond the scope of most electrical contractors without the assistance of an accountant or bookkeeper, you need to know how to apply the number to your estimate.

Calculation Methods

There are two methods of applying overhead to a job:

- Percentage-to-Prime Cost
- Cost per Labor Hour

2nd Printing

Most contractors apply overhead as a percentage of prime cost, but there is logic behind both methods. This topic is covered in greater detail in our Business Management program, but here is a brief explanation.

Percentage-to-Prime Cost

Most contractors apply overhead as a percentage of prime cost. This method has worked well for many contractors over many years, but it is most accurate when applied when the contractor does jobs that are similar in size and content.

For example, the percentage-to-prime cost method of applying overhead works well for a contractor who does strictly residential housing, or one that does only office buildouts.

This method should *not* be used by a contractor who does many different types of jobs such as residential, commercial, service, and so on, because the management demands are different for each type of job.

Since overhead is related primarily to the management of labor and not the cost of material, it should be applied to the labor man-hours of a job. We can calculate this value by dividing the overhead dollars for a given period of time by the actual field man-hours for the same period of time.

> **Word of Caution:** The percentage method is only suitable when it is being used on similar jobs where the ratio of material cost to labor cost is approximately the same from job to job.

Cost Per Labor Hour

If the jobs you are estimating are not approximately the same from job to job, you should consider using the cost per labor hour method. Calculating this is fairly straight forward. Take the total overhead dollars for a given period of time, and divide it by the actual field man-hours for the same period of time. The result will be your overhead cost per labor hour.

Understanding Electrical Estimating | MikeHolt.com

Review the following example:

 Cost Per Labor Hour Example

Labor hours for six months is 10,000 hours. If we know that our total overhead dollars for the same six months is $180,000, our overhead rate is $18 per hour.

Overhead Cost Per Labor Hour			
Month	Overhead Cost	Labor Hours	Cost Per Hour
April	$25,000	1,166	$21.44
May	$30,000	1,666	$18.01
June	$35,000	2,167	$16.51
July	$25,000	1,250	$20.00
August	$30,000	1,584	$18.94
September	$35,000	2,167	$16.51
Six Months	$180,000	10,000	$18.00

7.8 Break-Even Cost Review

Finally, we need to determine our break-even cost, or what we estimate it will cost to do the job. All you need to do is add the cost of labor, material, direct-job expenses, and overhead together.

Break-Even Cost = Labor + Material + Direct-Job Expenses + Overhead

The argument I hear at this point in my estimating classes is, "If I consider all of these factors and account for them in the estimate, I will never get a job!"

2nd Printing

Break Even Cost		
Labor Cost (109.77 hrs × $18/hr)		$1,975.86
Labor Burden (Included When Overhead is Applied)		$0.00
Material Cost		$2,278.20
Direct Job Cost		$550.00
Estimated Prime Cost		$4,804.06
Overhead ($18 per Labor Hour)	$18.00	$1,975.86
Break Even		$6,779.92

But let's slow down and remember what we are trying to accomplish—we are looking to determine our cost (the estimate). Once you know what you think it will cost you to cover all of your job costs (your break-even cost), you are welcome to make any business decision you want. But hopefully, you will not sell the job for less than you think it will cost you to complete it—just so you win the job. Remember we have not even added profit yet!

Final Thoughts

Once you know all of your job costs (the break-even point), every dollar above that is a dollar of profit—but every dollar below it is a dollar of loss.

It is worth noting that even one mistake in calculating the break-even point can be costly. Throughout the break-even analysis process, you will have to make judgment decisions on intangibles, such as job conditions, labor productivity, material requirements, waste, theft, small tools, direct-job expenses, and overhead.

The next chapter, The Bid Process, is where you take all the knowledge you have gained thus far and determine how much money you could make. This is the best part!

Understanding Electrical Estimating | MikeHolt.com

Use the information you learned in this chapter to answer the following questions.

Chapter 7—Review Questions

7.1 Introduction

1. The break-even-point of an estimate is the point where your bid price covers all ____.

   (a) job costs and overhead
   (b) permit fees
   (c) sales tax
   (d) labor costs

7.2 Break-Even Cost Summary Worksheet

2. When determining a job's break-even-point, the first step is to transfer the totals for ____ to a summary worksheet.

   (a) permit fees
   (b) sales tax
   (c) labor hours and material costs
   (d) consulting fees

3. The estimate summary worksheet has ____ major sections.

   (a) four
   (b) five
   (c) six
   (d) seven

4. Summary worksheets do not include a section for ____.

   (a) sales tax
   (b) labor hours
   (c) material cost
   (d) overhead

Understanding Electrical Estimating | Mike Holt Enterprises

Chapter 7

190

2nd Printing

7.3 Labor Hours and Labor Cost

5. Determining your break-even labor cost for the summary work-sheet requires you to adjust your ____ for working conditions based on a percentage for specific conditions.

    (a)   insurance costs
    (b)   labor hours
    (c)   profit margin
    (d)   travel time

6. After you have adjusted the total ____ for the break-even-cost, you must consider all necessary additional labor requirements for the job.

    (a)   material costs
    (b)   labor hours
    (c)   equipment costs
    (d)   insurance costs

7. As-built drawings that might be a factor in determining your break-even-cost, are intended to show, in accurate detail, the location of____.

    (a)   feeders
    (b)   branch circuits
    (c)   size of the electrical equipment
    (d)   all of these

8. Other items that might require additional labor requirements to be considered for the break-even-cost include ____.

    (a)   As-Built-Drawings
    (b)   Demolition
    (c)   Excavation
    (d)   all of these

9. Items that might require additional labor requirements to be considered for the break-even-cost include ____.

(a) Job location
(b) Public Safety
(c) Security
(d) all of these

10. The labor rate hour contributing to your break-even-cost can be determined by ____.

(a) The Bureau of Labor Statistics
(b) local and national averages
(c) shop and job averages
(d) prevailing wage rates

11. In addition to the cost of labor, there are other costs (labor burden) associated with labor that must be taken into consideration including ____

(a) payroll taxes
(b) worker's compensation
(c) employee benefits
(d) all of these

12. As of February 2024, the payroll taxes portion of your labor rate hour can be rounded off to approximately ____.

(a) 5 percent
(b) 8 percent
(c) 10 percent
(d) 12.5 percent

13. Workers' Compensation, unlike labor hour payroll taxes, is applied to total wages, and the cost should be between ____ of the total payroll.

(a) 5 and 10 percent
(b) 7 and 15 percent
(c) 10 and 12.5 percent
(d) 10 and 15 percent

14. Employee benefits contributing to the per hour labor rate should represent ____ at a minimum.

    (a)   10 percent
    (b)   15 percent
    (c)   20 percent
    (d)   25 percent

7.4 Material Cost

15. It is impractical to try to determine every material item required for a job such as routine "shop supplies" like mounting screws, pulling compound, wire connectors, tape, and so on. Add ____ of the material cost as a factor.

    (a)   3 percent
    (b)   5 percent
    (c)   8 percent
    (d)   10 percent

16. Costs for ladders and countless other small tools must be included in the estimate. A factor of ____ of the total material cost is considered an acceptable value for small tools.

    (a)   two percent
    (b)   three percent
    (c)   four percent
    (d)   five percent

17. Shrinkage is a term often used to describe the effects of waste and theft of material on the jobsite. For an efficiently managed job, ____ is reasonable

    (a)   two percent
    (b)   three percent
    (c)   four percent
    (d)   five percent

Understanding Electrical Estimating | MikeHolt.com

7.5 Direct-Job Expenses

18. Step 4 in determining the break-even cost is to account for ____.

    (a) vacation expenses
    (b) direct job expenses
    (c) trades meetings
    (d) licensing costs

19. Direct job expenses to be considered when determining your break-even-cost might include ____.

    (a) business and occupational fees
    (b) equipment rentals
    (c) permits and inspection fees
    (d) all of these

7.6 Estimated Prime Cost

20. ____ is a term used to identify the subtotaled cost of labor, material, and direct costs.

    (a) Estimated Prime Cost
    (b) Raw Costs
    (c) Job Subtotal
    (d) any of these

21. Calculating your estimated prime cost is just the simple matter of adding up the ____.

    (a) labor costs
    (b) material costs
    (c) direct job costs
    (d) all of these

7.7 Overhead

22. The cost related to the operation and management of the company is known as ____.

   (a)   overhead
   (b)   cost of doing business
   (c)   the operations budget
   (d)   municipal fees

23. The cost related to the operation and management of the company, such as ____ and so on, is known as overhead.

   (a)   rent
   (b)   vehicles
   (c)   administrative salaries
   (d)   all of these

7.8 Break-Even Cost Review

24. For the final step in determining your break-even-cost, all you need to do is add together the ____.

   (a)   cost of labor and materials
   (b)   direct job expenses
   (c)   overhead
   (d)   all of these

Understanding Electrical Estimating | MikeHolt.com

Notes...

2nd Printing

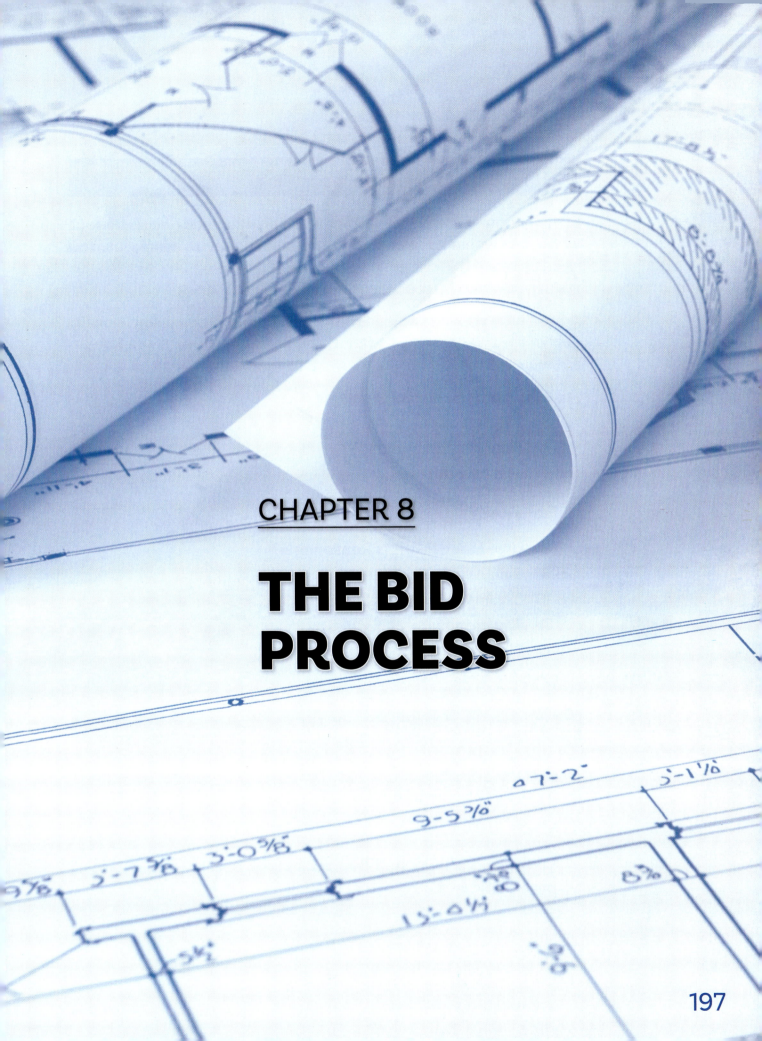

CHAPTER 8

THE BID PROCESS

8.1 Introduction

In this chapter, we will learn how to make an educated decision about when and where to spend our time and money to earn jobs. You need to make this decision early in the estimating process so that you don't waste time producing a bid for a job you shouldn't take.

Armed with your knowledge of the estimating process and how to determine the break-even point, you can learn how to prepare an accurate bid. Here's what we'll be considering:

8.2   **Listen to Your Gut Feelings**

8.3   **Job Selection**

8.4   **Financial Resources**

8.5   **Just Say No!**

8.6   **Understanding Bid Types**

8.7   **The Accurate Bid**

8.8   **How Much Profit Is Reasonable?**

8.9   **Calculating Bid Price**

8.10   **Bid Analysis**

8.11   **The Proposal**

8.12   **Closing the Deal**

8.2 Listen to Your Gut Feelings

Many electricians feel obligated to bid on a job, even when they don't think it's likely to be profitable.

> **Word of Caution:** If you don't think you are going to make money on the job, don't bid on it.

Remember why you are in business. It's better to be honest and up-front than to make excuses or pretend to be interested when you are not. Bidding on jobs when you can't make a profit just increases your overhead.

Before you expend any energy estimating a job:

- Research the individual or company. Run a credit check and talk with other trades or suppliers about their reputation for paying bills in a timely manner.
- Ask who did their electrical work in the past and try to determine why they are no longer doing the work.

You can't always prove that something is wrong. However, you don't always need proof to know that you should not take a certain job. Don't take a job if:

- They have unrealistic completion dates
- The jobsite concerns you
- The customer insists on a design that contains *Code* violations
- The plans are incomplete, and they say, "Trust me!"

If you get a bad feeling in your gut when you are in communication with a potential customer, it is a sign that something is not right. Trust your instincts and don't allow greed to override that feeling in your gut.

Make it a practice to only work for customers you like, who have a good reputation in the industry, and who respect you and your staff.

There is nothing wrong with telling a potential customer, "We don't wish to bid on this job." If you refuse to bid, you don't have to give a reason, even if they ask. It is not your place to teach them to be civil, to have a safe working environment, to behave ethically, or to correct whatever problem they have.

If they insist on a reason, just tell them it is not a good match between their needs and your company. Don't worry that you will be passing up potential income—you may just be passing up a significant loss.

Understanding Electrical Estimating | MikeHolt.com

8.3 Job Selection

Because there is always a limit to your energy, time, and money, you can't estimate all the jobs that are presented to you. Make sure to spend your time wisely by only bidding jobs that you have determined fit your business model. Ask yourself these questions before you decide to bid the work:

- Am I qualified to estimate this project?
- Are the contractor and/or owner's scheduling expectations realistic?
- Can I make money on this job?
- Can I manage this job so that it is profitable?
- Do I have enough time to properly estimate this job?
- Do I have the financial resources for this job?
- Do I have the proper tools and equipment to complete this job with profit?
- Do I have the workforce and skills to handle this job?
- Do I want the job?
- Do I want to work with this person or organization?
- What is the likelihood of winning the job if my price is competitive?
- What risk does this job present for our company?
- What does my gut say about this project or the contractor and/or owner?

You don't have to bid on every job that is offered, just bid on the ones that you believe you have a chance of winning while maintaining a profit margin that meets your needs.

Only bid jobs when the anticipated cash flow (speed of payment) provides the funds you need for payroll, material, and overhead when you need them.

8.4 Financial Resources

Don't become too excited about any particular job. You have worked too hard to get where you are to lose it all because the other party either did not pay you on time or didn't pay you at all.

Consider the financial effect of a job before you bid on it. If you can't financially manage it, then don't bid the job. The last thing you want is to have regrets!

> **Word of Caution:** It only takes one job to erase years of hard work and profit —or worse, sink your business!

Many contractors ignore this advice. If you are not convinced, make an appointment with a loan officer at your bank or your credit manager with your primary supplier to discuss general business and financial management. Be sure to ask, "What is the number one reason a business fails?"

The answer will be, "Failure to manage cash flow." If you do see a cash-flow crunch coming, talk to your banker before you need the money.

8.5 Just Say No!

If you have decided that you are not interested in bidding for a given job, immediately communicate this to the appropriate individual and remain firm in your decision.

Basically, it comes down to the reason an electrical contractor is in business, and that is to make as much money as possible while providing a valued service to your customer. You don't have to bid on every job offered, just bid on the ones that you believe you have a chance of winning while maintaining a profit margin that meets your needs.

Understanding Electrical Estimating | MikeHolt.com

TIP!

When you decline to bid for a job, consider giving the potential customer a competitor's telephone number. You will accomplish two things by this action: you will not waste your time, and you will keep your competitors busy with work you don't want.

8.6 Understanding Bid Types

Once you determine that bidding for a job is a good decision for your company, you need to figure out what type of bid to prepare and submit.

There are several types of bids an estimator may need to prepare including:

- Competitive Bid
- Design/Build Bid
- Negotiated Work and Guaranteed Maximum Price (GMP) Bid
- Time and Material (Cost Plus) Bid
- Unit Pricing Bid

Competitive Bid

Competitive bid work requires the contractor to submit a price, or a set of prices the company will charge to perform the services required in accordance with the drawings and specifications. This bid process requires competing contractors to submit bids, and the customer chooses from among them.

Customers often look at more than just the bid price. Factors that might be considered include a previous relationship, satisfaction with previous work, the contractor's attitude, the company's reputation, the company's experience relating to the work to be done, the technical approach of how the specified work will be completed in the time required, and whether the company has adequate resources to complete the project in a timely manner. Many contractors like this type of bidding because everything is laid out, so everyone is bidding on the "same page." Efficiency and organization on the jobsite ultimately determine profitability.

Design/Build Bid

Design/build bids require the electrical contractor to design and construct the electrical wiring according to written specifications. To be successful with design/build bids, the electrical contractor must know the customer's needs and the *National Electrical Code*.

Negotiated Work and Guaranteed Maximum Price (GMP) Bid

Negotiated work is an agreement between the electrical contractor and the customer on the scope of the job and how much it will cost. These are often accompanied by a Guaranteed Maximum Price (GMP).

This type of work relies on past performance (honesty, quality of service, and professionalism), and a secure long-term relationship with the customer to have the opportunity to negotiate the price of an upcoming project.

This is a fragile, but lucrative market, which can be maintained only when the electrical contractor is honest in pricing and provides outstanding service that meets or exceeds the customer's expectations. Maintaining these types of clients requires a high level of record keeping and client interaction.

Understanding Electrical Estimating | MikeHolt.com

Time and Material (Cost Plus) Bid

Time and material pricing is often used when job conditions make it impossible to provide a fixed-dollar bid. In its simplest form, price is based on a given rate per labor hour with the material billed at an agreed markup amount (such as 20 percent above cost).

This type of work carries a lower risk with a low-profit margin. It sometimes has a "not-to-exceed" price clause that increases the risk to the contractor, typically with a larger profit margin. This type of work is often used for change orders, especially when a job is over budget.

While some contractors consider this type of work as their "bread and butter," it is more stressful than others because the customer is more likely to question the amount of time for which you bill. It is best to restrict this to customers with whom you have a long-term relationship (trust).

Also remember that when you do this type of work, it is usually because you are reducing profit in order to reduce risk. Adding a "not-to-exceed" clause adds the risk factor back into the work. But the very low profit margin remains, although the risk of accepting such a clause can be reduced when you use unit pricing, which we will discuss shortly.

Estimate this type of work as best you can, and then stick with the numbers you reached.

Unit Pricing Bid

Some jobs are awarded on the basis of unit pricing. Unit pricing is the price to install a given electrical component, such as a switch, receptacle, or paddle fan. It also includes the cost of labor, material, overhead, and profit.

Unit pricing is used for almost all types of construction such as renovations, office buildouts, change orders, and so on. This type of bid requires confidence and job experience, because a wrong unit price, when extended, will multiply the error.

> **Word of Caution:** A mistake in a unit price calculation will be multiplied by the number of times the unit is used on the project!

Requests for unit pricing are sometimes included in the specifications, or in add/deduct options—especially with commercial and residential work.

Governmental work sometimes consists of an entire (thick) document consisting of nothing but unit pricing items. The low bidder receives a contract for all of the work for a year.

Once you receive an order for work to be performed, you can negotiate the price of any additional work/material necessary for "missing" items such as additional wire for a circuit that must be added because of the number of additional fixtures, receptacles, and/or switches being ordered.

8.7 The Accurate Bid

High bids can cause you to lose the sales that your company depends on. Low bids can win sales but cause the loss of profits or the demise of the company. Between these two losing propositions is the "accurate" bid—and that is the only kind of bid you want to produce.

An accurate bid is important and:

- Helps quantify profits
- Eliminates accidental built-in loss of revenue or profit
- Provides a means of knocking low bids out of the competition
- Reduces cash flow problems
- Reduces resource conflicts
- Provides the highest return on the bidding effort
- Provides accurate information for negotiation to win a job or support changes
- Reduces risk

Understanding Electrical Estimating | MikeHolt.com

Bid Review

To ensure that your bid is accurate, you need to verify the following:

- Device grade requirement: General Use/Hospital/Specification
- "Construction" math and financial calculations
- Jobsite conditions, especially for retrofit/remodel jobs
- Specification and/or drawing notes
- Fixture, gear, and/or subcontractor quote matches plan counts and specs
- Site/underground work requirements included
- All plan sections "colored in"
- Copies of supplier quotes on file
- The correct scale used for drawing takeoffs
- Labor unit totals and material cost totals pass the "sniff" test

> Many people think a winning bid is the one that lands the job, but the winning bid is the **most accurate** bid.

The Winning Bid

It is important that you understand what a "winning bid" actually is—it's the one that's the most accurate.

Quite often, the company that lands the job is actually the "losing" bid, because the company that won the job by underbidding due to inaccuracy in their estimate. Conversely an accurately estimated bid:

- Provides work that your company can handle
- Gives you an opportunity to make money
- Prevents you from taking on unprofitable work
- Builds rapport with your customers

A poorly estimated bid:

- Puts you at risk with work that you might not be able to handle
- Can prevent you from taking on profitable work
- Can damage your customer relationships and your reputation
- Can put you out of business

Other Considerations

Here are a few other items to carefully consider before you submit a proposal to your customer to make sure you have an accurate bid.

Review the plans and specifications one final time before submitting your bid, and make sure you understand all of the bid conditions. Make sure you consider the following before submitting a bid:

- Completion Penalty
- Finance Cost
- Liquidated Damages
- Retainage Cost

Completion Penalty

Some projects may have penalties such as $500 to $1,000 for each day past the scheduled completion date, essentially a punishment for not being done on time. You need to consider these costs when you determine your final bid price.

Look at the anticipated job schedule and your list of specialty items, such as switchgear, panels, a generator, lighting fixtures, or other items that will likely need to be specially ordered. Find out from the vendors what the anticipated lead time is, and allow some time for the submittal and approval process, perhaps a month.

Now look at where the delivery dates fall within the job schedule. Will there be sufficient time to install the items before the scheduled completion date? It may be worthwhile to put a qualification in your proposal about an availability issue related to the job schedule.

Finance Cost

Be sure to include the cost to finance the job if this is applicable. For example, the cost of borrowing $25,000 at an interest rate of 10 percent for a year is $2,500.

Understanding Electrical Estimating | MikeHolt.com

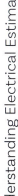

Liquidated Damages

The most common component of a liquidated damage clause is the calculated cost to the owner arising from each day of delay. That amount is then set forth in the bidding and contract documents.

Some documents may limit the owner to recovering a specific amount; some allow for complete recovery if the calculated amount falls short. Also, in cases where there has been blatant disregard by a contractor to perform, the owner may file a suit for additional damages.

It is important to pay close attention to the verbiage of liquidated damage clauses. In the courts, liquidated damages cases have not been dealt with in a consistent manner. In the United States, the courts have tended not to enforce the Liquidated Damages clause if the stipulated amount exceeds the actual loss but have required compensation for the actual harm suffered.

> This value might be insignificant to some, but somebody is going to pay for this. Then again, it might already have been included when you applied overhead.

Retainage Cost

Some jobs require that a portion of each payment (typically 10 percent) be held for a specific period of time (typically 90 to 180 days) after the final electrical inspection. Some require a portion be held for the duration of your warranty period.

The purpose of the owner holding back the money (retainage), is to guarantee that the electrical system has been installed correctly and according to the contract before all final payments have been released.

You might want to add the cost of money you do not have access to.

Cost of Money Example: Retainage cost (10%) for 180 days for a $250,000 project will be $1,500 at an interest rate of 12 percent.

Cost = ($250,000 × 10%) × (12% × 0.50)

Cost = ($25,000) × (6%)

Cost = $1,500 or 0.01% of the selling price

8.8 How Much Profit Is Reasonable?

Net profit is the bottom line. It is a report card against which all businesspersons are measured. A winning bid includes a reasonable amount for profit.

A reasonable profit margin will be whatever the market will bear—without gouging the customer.

Some factors to consider include:

- Competition and Economy
- Management/Organization
- Job Size
- Risk
- Speed of Payment

Competition and Economy

Consider the number of competitors who are expected to be bidding on the job and their experience in the particular line of work.

When the construction market is in a recession, or the market is shrinking, a highly competitive market develops and competition for jobs drives the selling price down.

If the economy is strong, or the market is expanding, prices and profits typically increase. This all happens according to the law of supply and demand. Consider increasing your profit margins when you are busy and lowering them when you are slow. Sometimes it is just that simple.

Understanding Electrical Estimating | MikeHolt.com

Management/Organization

Profitable contracting demands that the job be sold for more than it will cost to complete it. To meet this goal, manage your resources efficiently and keep your costs down. If you do, your prices should be competitive, even with a profit margin exceeding that of your competitors.

Job Size

The generally accepted practice is that smaller jobs are sold with higher profit margins as compared to larger jobs. This may not be the case in specialized markets. Know your market so you don't "leave money on the table" when you submit a bid.

Risk

When doing an unfamiliar job, you might need to increase your profit margin to cover the risk of completing the project within the price of the estimate. However, the risk factor might not be the same for your competitors, thus allowing them to submit a lower bid.

Speed of Payment

Consider how quickly you are likely to be paid. If there is likely to be an extended amount of time involved, then you might need to consider the cost of financing your investment in the job.

8.9 Calculating Bid Price

Profit to Break-Even Cost

Most contractors apply profit as a percentage of the break-even cost, so be sure to use a markup multiplier, not the percent of profit to sales value from the financial statement!

Smaller-Sized Contractor Income Statement Year Ending December 31		
Sales	$250,000	100% of Sales
Direct Job Cost		
Labor (4,000 Hrs)	$80,000	
Material	$70,000	
Total Direct Cost	$150,000	60% of Sales
Gross Profit	$100,000	40% of Sales
Overhead Expenses (Administrative Cost)		
Salaries and Commissions	$15,000	
Advertising	$5,000	
Auto and Gas	$10,000	
Benefits	$20,000	
Interest	$1,000	
Insurance—Auto, General, Workers' Comp.	$5,000	
Miscellaneous Expense	$3,000	
Payroll Taxes	$8,000	
Rent	$5,000	
Utilities/Phone	$3,000	
Total Administrative Expenses (50% of Prime)	$75,000	30% of Sales
Net Profit Before Taxes (16.67% of Prime)	$25,000	10% of Sales

Understanding Electrical Estimating | MikeHolt.com

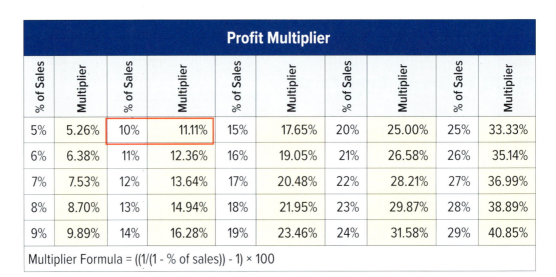

Profit Multiplier

% of Sales	Multiplier	% of Sales	Multiplier	% of Sales	Multiplier	% of Sales	Multiplier	% of Sales	Multiplier
5%	5.26%	10%	11.11%	15%	17.65%	20%	25.00%	25%	33.33%
6%	6.38%	11%	12.36%	16%	19.05%	21%	26.58%	26%	35.14%
7%	7.53%	12%	13.64%	17%	20.48%	22%	28.21%	27%	36.99%
8%	8.70%	13%	14.94%	18%	21.95%	23%	29.87%	28%	38.89%
9%	9.89%	14%	16.28%	19%	23.46%	24%	31.58%	29%	40.85%

Multiplier Formula = ((1/(1 - % of sales)) - 1) × 100

Profit

Description	Value	To Sales
Labor Cost	$1,975.86	26.23%
Labor Burden (Included When Overhead is Applied)	$0.00	0.00%
Material Cost	$2,278.20	30.24%
Direct Job Cost	$550.00	7.30%
Estimated Prime Cost	$4,804.06	63.77%
Overhead, (Hrs × Rate per Hour)	$1,975.86	26.23%
Break Even	$6,779.92	90.00%
Profit 10% of Sales (Markup 11.11%)	$753.25	10.00%
Bid Price	$7,533.17	100.00%

Calculating Markup—Profit Multiplier Example:
What is 10 percent margin (markup) with a job having a job cost of $6,779.92?

Bid Price = Break-Even Cost + (Break-Even Cost x Multiplier %)
Bid Price = $6,779.92 + ($6,779.92 x 11.11%)
Bid Price = $6,779.92 + $753.25
Bid Price = $7,533.17

Calculating Markup—Profit Markup Example: What is 10 percent margin (markup) with a job having a job cost of $6,779.92?

Bid Price = Break-Even Cost / (100% - Markup %)

Bid Price = $6,779.92 (Cost) / (100% - 10%)
Bid Price = $6,779.92 / 90%
Bid Price = $7,533.17

Submitted Bid Price	
Labor Costs	
Labor Cost (Hours × Rate) (109.77 × $18.00)	$1,975.86
Labor Burden (Included when overhead is applied)	$0.00
Material Cost	$2,278.20
Direct Job Cost	$550.00
Estimated Prime Cost	$4,804.06
Overhead (Hours × Rate per Hour)	$1,975.86
Break Even	$6,779.92
Profit 10% of Sales (Markup multiplier 11.11%)	$753.25
Bid Price	$7,533.17
Other Bid Considerations	
Completion Penalty Allowance	$0.00
Finance Cost (part of overhead)	$0.00
Liquidated Damages Allowance	$0.00
Retainage Cost Allowance	$0.00
Other Costs	$0.00
Submitted Bid Price	**$7,533.17**

Understanding Electrical Estimating | MikeHolt.com

8.10 Bid Analysis

Before submitting your bid to the customer, do as much bid analysis as possible to ensure your price is as accurate as possible and nothing falls through the cracks.

The following techniques can be used to check various parts of your bid very quickly as a sniff test:

- Branch-Circuit Check
- Percentage of Distribution Check
- Cost per Square Foot
- Cost per Labor Hour
- Labor Days
- Experience

If something seems off, go back and double check your work.

Branch-Circuit Check

A quick check worth doing is to divide the total footage of branch-circuit raceways by the number of outlets. This type of analysis can be applied to each phase of a project such as fire alarm systems, sound systems, and so forth.

Average Branch Circuit Length per Outlet			
Outlets		**Branch Raceways**	
Fluorescent Fixtures	18	1/2 EMT 2—12 AWG	662
Recessed Lights	24	1/2 EMT 3—12 AWG	91
Exit Lights	2	1/2 EMT 4—12 AWG	128
Switch Outlets	4	1/2 EMT 5—12 AWG	10
Receptacle Outlet	9	Total 1/2 EMT	891
IG Receptacle Outlet	2		
Total	**59**	**Run per Outlet**	**15.10**

Another quick check is to divide branch-circuit wiring by branch-circuit raceway lengths. If the answer is less than 2 or more than 4, that is a warning sign to check for errors.

Avg. # of Wires per Raceway Ft	
Branch Raceways	
1/2 EMT 2—12 AWG	662
1/2 EMT 3—12 AWG	91
1/2 EMT 4—12 AWG	128
1/2 EMT 5—12 AWG	10
Total 1/2 EMT	891
Run per Outlet	15.10
12 AWG	2,393
Average per EMT Ft	**2.69**

Percentage of Distribution Check

Check the percentage distribution of labor, material, direct cost, overhead, and profit to sales. Be sure you do this for all jobs so that you can compare each bid against previously completed jobs of a similar nature.

Percent Distribution to Selling Price		
Description	**Value**	**To Sales**
Labor Cost	$1,975.86	26.23%
Labor Burden (Included When Overhead is Applied)	$0.00	0.00%
Material Cost	$2,278.20	30.24%
Direct Job Cost	$550.00	7.30%
Estimated Prime Cost	$4,804.06	63.77%
Overhead, (Hrs × Rate per Hour)	$1,975.86	26.23%
Break Even	$6,779.92	90.00%
Profit 10% of Sales (Markup 11.11%)	$753.25	10.00%
Bid Price	**$7,533.17**	**100.00%**

Understanding Electrical Estimating | MikeHolt.com

Cost per Square Foot

Another check is to calculate the cost per square foot. Simply divide the selling price by the square footage of the building. The cost per square foot values can be used to check an estimate for validity, not as the basis for a bid.

Cost per Square Foot Example: What is the cost per square foot for a 2,500 sq ft meeting room with a bid price of $7,533.17?

Bid Cost sq ft = Bid Price / Square Foot
Bid Cost sq ft = $7,533.17 / 2,500 sq ft
Bid Cost sq ft = $3.01 sq ft

Cost per Labor Hour

Another check is to calculate the cost per labor hour. Simply divide the selling price by the number of labor hours. The cost per labor hour values can be used to check an estimate for validity, not as the basis for a bid.

Cost per Labor Hour Example: What is the cost per labor hour for a 2,500 sq ft meeting room with a bid price of $7,533.17 and 109.77 hours of labor?

Bid Cost per Labor Hour = Bid Price/Labor Hours
Bid Cost per Labor Hour = $7,533.17 / 109.77 hours
Bid Cost per Labor Hour = $68.63

Labor Days

One final consideration is how the job will be staffed (number of man-days) and if this information appears to be valid. You determine this by dividing the total job hours by the number of hours per day that the job will be staffed.

Labor Days Example: How many labor days are needed to complete a meeting room, estimated to take 109.77 hours and using two electricians?

Labor Days = Job Labor Hours / (Number of Electricians x Hours per Day)

Labor Days = 109.77 hours / (2 Electricians x 8 hrs)
Labor Days = 109.77 hours / 16 hrs
Labor Days = 6.86 days

Experience

These were just a few examples of quick checks you can make to a bid before you send it to the customer. With experience, an esti-mator will develop their skills and accumulate historical data allowing them to quickly check bids for errors.

8.11 The Proposal

When the bid is complete, you must submit a written proposal that clarifies what the bid includes *and* what it does not. The following is a sample of what your proposal might look like:

Understanding Electrical Estimating | MikeHolt.com

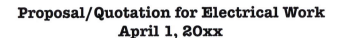

Proposal/Quotation for Electrical Work
April 1, 20xx

Owner/Contractor
Mike Holt Enterprises, Inc.
3604 Parkway Blvd. Suite 3
Leesburg, Florida 34748
352-360-2620 (c), 352-360-0983 (f)

Project Location
3604 Parkway Blvd., Suite 3
Leesburg, Florida 34748

Scope of Work
Wire meeting room as per drawing and supply all electrical fixtures and wiring devices as per the following:

Fixtures

Fluorescent Lay-In	18
Recessed	24
Exit	2

Switches

Switch—Single Pole (1-Gang)	1
Switch—3-Way (1-Gang)	1
Switch—Two Single-Pole (2-Gang)	1
Switch—One Single-Pole & One 3-Way (2-Gang)	1

Receptacles

Receptacle 20A, 125V	9
Receptacle IG 20A, 125V	2
Total Outlets	59
Cost	
	$7,533.17

Terms and Conditions

Plans/Specifications. Electrical work requested by others not indicated on plans and/or specifications shall not be part of this agreement.

Change Orders. Deviation or alteration to the scope of this agreement, including plans or specifications, shall be executed on receipt of written orders.

Design Errors. Wiring modifications required because of errors in design by the architect and/or engineer shall be considered a change order.

Equipment Supplied by Others. Electrical Contractor shall not be responsible for the installation, damage, theft, vandalism, storage, or warranty of equipment supplied by others.

Codes and Installation Practices. Material and equipment supplied by Electrical Contractor shall be installed in accordance with the *National Electrical Code*, local electrical building code, and standard electrical practices. Requirements that are not codified as of the date of this proposal are excluded from this quotation.

Payment and Terms. Payment(s) not received according to an approved payment schedule shall be considered past due, and Electrical Contractor will not perform any work until all past-due payments are current.

Performance. Electrical Contractor will not work after 5 p.m. or weekends (overtime) unless authorized in writing by owner/contractor via a signed change order.

Permit. The cost of the permit shall be paid by owner.

Repairs. Electrical Contractor shall not be responsible for any work associated with the repair of concrete/drywall, including painting, patching, and sealing of roof penetrations as required for the installation of electrical wiring and equipment.

Temporary Power. None to be supplied by Electrical Contractor.

Termination of Agreement. This agreement shall remain in effect for 365 days from the date of signing of this agreement by the owner/contractor and Electrical Contractor.

Warranty. The warranty of electrical material and equipment supplied by Electrical Contractor shall be for a period of one year from the date of final invoice. No warranty will be provided for material and equipment supplied by others, and no warranty shall be performed while invoice(s), including change order(s) are past due.

Waste. Electrical Contractor supplied waste shall be removed to a specific area on the construction site as instructed by the owner/contractor.

This proposal/quotation does not become legal and binding unless signed by both parties.

_____ Date: _____/_____/_____
Owner/Contractor

_____ Date: _____/_____/_____
Mike Holt Enterprises, Inc.

Understanding Electrical Estimating | MikeHolt.com

It's common for a proposal to go back and forth between the parties to accommodate various little details for the customer's satisfaction. Make sure that you *never* send a proposal over that you have pre-signed.

If you do that, the customer can make changes that you have not seen or reviewed or approved, and then send it back with their signature. That makes for a difficult conversation with your customer and maybe a lawyer if something goes wrong. Instead, wait until the customer has reviewed, changed, and signed the proposal before giving it a final review and countersigning it.

Word of Caution: Never pre-sign a proposal before sending to the customer.

8.12 Closing the Deal

Once the proposal has been sent, it's time to close the deal. Sometimes, there's nothing to do but wait, but in many cases, it's time to touch base with the customer.

TIP! A short phone call or meeting to review the bid details and ensure everything is what they requested and understood will go a long way toward winning the job. Remember, it's not always about the lowest price.

The Contract

Contract review is outside this program's scope, but it's important! Once you have been awarded a contract, it's time to get busy. You must have the business skills to handle contract paperwork and start managing the job. Make sure you take the time to get educated about contractor business skills if you are the one who is responsible for carrying the process forward.

Final Thoughts

Congratulations! So far in this program you have traded guesswork for methodology, risk for opportunity, and uncertainty for confidence.

You have come a long way in a short time. At this point, you have seen how to produce an estimate, determine the break-even point, and develop a bid. You have methods that will allow you to do those things accurately, efficiently, and thoroughly. With hard work and dedication, your reputation should grow right along with your company's profits.

Understanding Electrical Estimating | MikeHolt.com

Use the information you learned in this chapter to answer the following questions.

Chapter 8—Review Questions

8.2 Listen to Your Gut Feelings

1.   Many electricians feel obligated to bid a job, even when it is not likely to be profitable. If you don't think you are going to make money on the job, ____.

(a)   over bid it to compensate in case you get the job
(b)   better to lose money than a customer
(c)   don't bid on it
(d)   try to negotiate

8.3 Job Selection

2.   Because there is a limit to your time and energy. prior to bidding a particular job, ask yourself ____.

(a)   am I qualified to estimate this project
(b)   are the scheduling expectations realistic
(c)   is this job profitable
(d)   all of these

3.   Other things you should ask yourself prior to bidding a particular job are, do I have ____.

(a)   enough time to properly estimate the job
(b)   the financial resources for this job
(c)   the proper tools and equipment
(d)   all of these

8.4 Financial Resources

4. Consider the financial effect of a job before you bid it. If you can't financially manage it, then ____.

    (a) verify your lines of credit
    (b) seek out a construction loan
    (c) don't bid it
    (d) collaborate with another contractor

8.5 Just Say No!

5. If you have decided that you are not interested in bidding a given job, immediately communicate this to the appropriate individual and ____.

    (a) give a reason
    (b) remain firm in your decision
    (c) try to negotiate better terms or conditions
    (d) any of these

8.6 Understanding Bid Types

6. ____ bid work requires the contractor to submit a price, or a set of prices the company will charge, to perform the services required in accordance with the drawings and specifications.

    (a) Competitive
    (b) Design/build
    (c) Negotiated
    (d) Time and material

7. ____ bids require the electrical contractor to design and construct the electrical wiring according to written specifications.

    (a) Competitive
    (b) Design/build
    (c) Negotiated
    (d) Time and material

8. To be successful with design/build bids, the electrical contractor must know the customer's needs and the _____.

(a) local ordinances
(b) *National Electrical Code*
(c) OSHA Standards
(d) International Construction Code

9. _____ work is an agreement between the electrical contractor and the customer on the scope of the job and how much it will cost.

(a) Competitive
(b) Design/build
(c) Negotiated
(d) Time and material

10. _____ pricing is often used when job conditions make it impossible to provide a fixed-dollar bid. In its simplest form, price is based on a given rate per labor hour with the material billed at an agreed markup amount.

(a) Competitive
(b) Design/build
(c) Negotiated
(d) Time and material

11. Time and material pricing is based on a given rate per labor hour with the material billed at an agreed markup amount like _____ above cost for example.

(a) 5 percent
(b) 20 percent
(c) 30 percent
(d) 50 percent

12. Unit pricing is the price to install a given electrical component, such as a switch, receptacle, or paddle fan. It also includes the cost of labor and _____.

(a) material
(b) overhead
(c) profit
(d) all of these

2nd Printing

13. ____ is(are) used for almost all types of construction such as renovations, office build-outs, change orders, and so on.

    (a) Competitive bids
    (b) Negotiated bids
    (c) Time and material bids
    (d) Unit pricing

8.7 The Accurate Bid

14. Accurate bidding a job is important because it ____.

    (a) helps quantify profits
    (b) provides a means of knocking low bids out of the competition
    (c) provides the highest return on the bidding effort
    (d) all of these

15. When reviewing your bid, to ensure that your bid is accurate, you need to verify ____.

    (a) device grade requirements
    (b) jobsite conditions
    (c) all supplier quotes match the plan counts and specs
    (d) all of these

16. Many people think that a winning bid is the one that lands the job, but the winning bid is actually the ____.

    (a) cheapest bid
    (b) most accurate bid
    (c) one in the middle
    (d) most expensive bid

17. Other considerations for bid accuracy are ____.

    (a) completion penalties
    (b) finance costs
    (c) retainage costs
    (d) all of these

Understanding Electrical Estimating | MikeHolt.com

8.8 How Much Profit Is Reasonable?

18.   ____ is a (are a) factor(s) to consider when determining a reasonable profit margin.

(a)   Competition and economy
(b)   Job size
(c)   Risk
(d)   all of these

19.   Also affecting profit margin, is when the construction market is in a recession, or the market is shrinking, a ____ market develops and competition for jobs drives the selling price down

(a)   buyers
(b)   sellers
(c)   highly competitive
(d)   depressed

8.9 Calculating Bid Price

20.   When calculating the bid price, most contractors apply profit as a percentage of the____.

(a)   labor and material cost
(b)   break-even cost
(c)   cost of goods sold
(d)   cost of doing business

8.10 Bid Analysis

21.   Before submitting your bid to the customer, do as much bid analysis as possible to ensure your price is as ____ as possible and nothing falls through the cracks.

(a)   profitable
(b)   accurate
(c)   risk-free
(d)   appealing

22. A quick check to perform as a part of your bid analysis is to complete a ____.

    (a) branch-circuit check
    (b) percentage of distribution check
    (c) cost per square foot check
    (d) any of these

23. When performing a percentage of distribution check, check the percentage distribution of ____ relative to sales.

    (a) labor, material, direct job cost
    (b) overhead
    (c) profit
    (d) all of these

8.11 The Proposal

24. When the bid is complete, you must submit a(an) ____ proposal that clarifies what the bid includes and what it does not.

    (a) verbal
    (b) sealed
    (c) written
    (d) electronic

25. Your written proposal should include the ____.

    (a) scope of work
    (b) terms
    (c) conditions
    (d) all of these

26. The terms and conditions of your proposal should include provisions for ____.

    (a) change orders
    (b) design errors
    (c) payment terms
    (d) all of these

Notes...

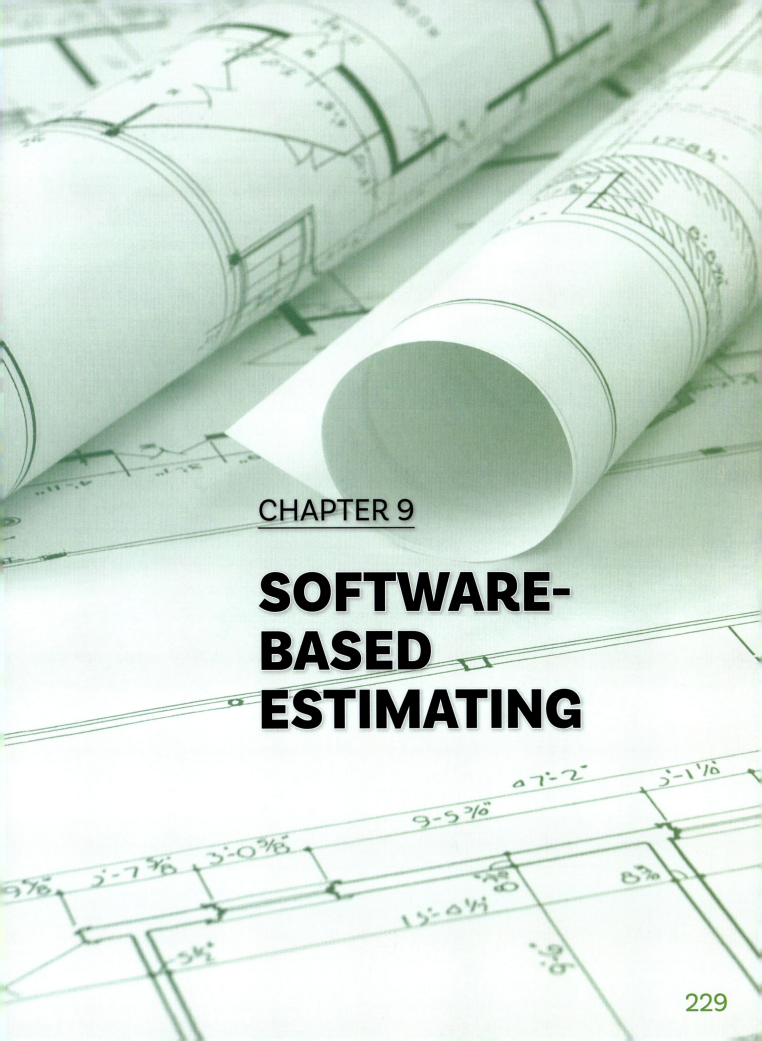

CHAPTER 9

SOFTWARE-BASED ESTIMATING

9.1 Introduction

Previous chapters have focused on concepts related to manual estimating. This chapter will give you an overview of how to use these same methods along with technology to become a better estimator.

Remember, software does have its limits and cannot replace your judgment, experience, or knowledge of the type of electrical installation you are estimating. We cover:

- 9.2   **Estimating Software**
- 9.3   **Backup System**
- 9.4   **Can I Afford It?**
- 9.5   **Material Pricing Services**

9.2 Estimating Software

There are a number of things to consider when learning about estimating software. Most of these topics are relevant to every situation, so take your time as you review each of the following items and make sure you are honest with yourself about what you really need.

Selection

Creating an accurate estimate requires great attention to detail and a specific set of tasks to be completed in order. The key to success in software-based estimating is taking the time to select software that meets your needs.

You have two basic choices when selecting estimating software: a spreadsheet or a software suite.

Spreadsheets

Spreadsheets are appropriate if you don't bid on larger jobs. They have been used for unit pricing, change orders, and simple jobs for years and may be just what you need.

Be careful, while they are an excellent solution for small jobs, don't try to get into the software business. You wouldn't send a motor and pulleys to a jobsite and tell the foreman to build a wire puller, so don't do it with estimating software.

He may get it done, but does it make economic sense? Such an approach will ultimately cost you more than what you will spend by investing in the right software package.

The spreadsheet method can become overwhelmingly complex as you try to scale upward. With an estimating software package, you have many advantages over the homegrown spreadsheet approach. To see these advantages, ask an estimating sales representative for a demonstration and a trial of their product.

Set Up and Training

Once you have selected a software and before you start entering data, you need to learn to use it! Training can require hours to days, so take the time to carefully select the right software and the right software vendor to partner with.

Regardless of how well estimating software is designed, do not expect optimum results without complete training. Professional training is best done away from the office. Attempting to have training in your office during business hours is usually a fiasco due to interruptions from other employees, phone calls, and unexpected visitors.

Be prepared to devote serious time to learning how to use this new tool. It will be extremely difficult to learn new software at the same time as you are trying to estimate multiple projects.

Instead, try to devote extra hours of training after work or on the weekends. The more time you put into using the program, the faster you will master it.

During your negotiations with the software vendor, ask if they will provide the training necessary at no additional cost. Some will, others will not—but it never hurts to ask!

> **Word of Caution:** If you attempt to use your software without proper training, you may never learn all of the valuable features that are designed within the program. Worse, you are likely to set things up in ways that will work against you, and probably establish bad practices from the outset. Avoid those problems by knowing what you are doing *before* you get knee deep into using this new tool.

This is a critical component of making money. Don't take any chances.

Technical Support

Software is not a one-time expense; it carries a continuous cost for annual support. Be sure you can count on long-term service from the company and that they will give you close personal attention.

Verify the costs for customer support and the hours they are available for phone and/or e-mail support. If you are going to have multiple systems, or have a multi-user network version, find out if it will be a single location or "per seat" annual fee. These fees and services can cost as much as a single-user license but can pay for themselves over the course of a year—especially when a technician helps you restore a job file an hour before a bid is due!

Database

A standard computer-assisted estimating system requires the estimator to take the time to learn how it works and requires effort to build the right items and assemblies in the database.

The additional information required by computer-assisted estimating systems considers the type of construction. Conversely, the manual-counting method uses an accepted figure regardless of the construction type. However, once an assembly is built, it can be used repeatedly (as long as prices are updated), and this will speed up the estimating process.

Most systems will have a database of parts and assemblies included in the software product, but someone must take time to verify the assemblies, material prices, and labor units. Once verified, a well set up database can increase the speed and accuracy of the takeoff.

Someone must assign the proper breakout or section of the bid prior to entering data. A "count entry" function requires typing in and/or clicking a button for the correct value. This can be more work than handwriting a symbol or note, and then placing a figure underneath it.

Takeoffs

Some estimators will still use the manual takeoff to a paper system, and then enter the information into the computer. Since computer-based estimating shares most of the takeoff steps with manual estimating, this method works well.

Other estimators will take advantage of on-screen-takeoff and store the digital plans for future reference. Most computer-based estimating supports all three types of takeoffs in some form:

- Manual Takeoff
- Direct Takeoff
- Automatic On-Screen Takeoff (OST)

Time Savings

The amount of time saved depends on the software, estimator, and complexity of the jobs being estimated. As the estimator becomes more familiar with the system, efficiency improves, and the time to do a given task decreases. The more complicated the job, the more the software can save you time by removing grunt work.

Understanding Electrical Estimating | MikeHolt.com

Improved Accuracy

The manual method requires a detailed write-up and expansion of the counted items. For example, a duplex receptacle has at least nine individual components which need to be written down, along with their associated material prices and labor units. Calculate these values against the quantities and enter subtotals for each. After all this, final totals need to be summed up.

This takes a great deal of time, effort, accuracy, and hand strength. After all this, someone else will need to double-check the extensions for accuracy. Imagine the time required to complete this process on a bid that has three or more bid forms. Worse, imagine what has to be done if something changes or a mistake is found after these final extensions are created.

Manual Extensions						
Item Description	Qty	Cost	Ext Cost	Labor Hours	Ext Hours	Unit
Metal Boxes 4 × 4" Regular	1	$47.84	$0.48	18.00	0.18	100
Rings, 1-Gang	1	$39.00	$0.39	4.50	0.05	100
EMT Set Screw Connectors ½"	2	$9.43	$0.19	2.00	0.04	100
EMT ½"	20	$19.39	$3.88	2.25	0.45	100
EMT Set Screw Couplings ½"	1	$9.70	$0.10	2.00	0.02	100
EMT Straps 1-Hole ½"	3	$3.10	$0.09	2.50	0.08	100
Switches—15A, 125V, 1-Pole	1	$58.23	$0.58	20.00	0.20	100
Plates, Plastic 1-Gang Switch	1	$18.88	$0.19	2.50	0.03	100
Wire—12 THHN, Copper, 600V	50	$73.69	$3.68	4.25	0.21	1,000
Totals			$9.58		1.26	

Software can help improve accuracy quite a bit, particularly during the extension phase of your estimates. The computer does the calculations with more accuracy and speed than any human (or even a large group of humans) ever could. If something changes or a mistake is found, it is much easier to make the necessary corrections and redo the extensions.

Remember, a computer does not make mistakes, it does not get tired, it does not forget the data when distractions occur, it does not omit steps in calculations, and it does not make errors in overlooking taxes, overhead, or profit!

Software can help improve accuracy quite a bit, particularly during the extension phase of your estimates. But if you do not enter the data for your estimate accurately, you will not have an accurate bid.

Quality

If you succeed in accurate count and entry, your estimates should be more complete than any done manually. Computer-based estimates also contain information to increase efficiency and improve profit margins.

Adaptation

Most software will be flexible and adapt to your estimating style, but do not expect it to fit *all* your habits perfectly. You will be required to "tweak" your system to be efficient.

Item Entry and Takeoff

Much like a manual takeoff, an accurate computer-based takeoff relies on a repeatable process that is consistent from start to finish. One advantage of computer-based takeoff is that the software design usually pushes you through the estimating process in a logical sequence.

Once mastered, a direct takeoff on a computer is a huge time-saver. It improves accuracy and reduces your chances of making mistakes in half by eliminating the need to write the count and takeoff information on a spreadsheet.

Understanding Electrical Estimating | MikeHolt.com

Bid Analysis

As you begin to use software to estimate your jobs, make sure that you carefully analyze and check each bid number. You will need to be able to replicate the manual adjustments that you have made to your labor units and add costs, overhead, and profit in the same way you did on the manual estimate that you produce.

Reduced Risk

Estimating software does not eliminate the need to learn how to estimate, but it can make a good estimator far more effective by eliminating human error. Reduced error results in reduced risk and an opportunity to make more money!

Time Management

We have already discussed that spending money on technology is a way to trade money for more time. A computer does thousands of mathematical computations in a fraction of a second, never makes a mathematical error, never becomes tired or careless, and never forgets. This is a path to recover your most valuable asset–time!

Some functions that are significantly improved by using a computer-estimating system include:

- Reduced estimating time and costs
- No errors when manually pricing, laboring, extending, or totaling
- Additional time can be used for bid review or additional estimates
- Highly organized and easily accessible bid and estimate history
- You can spend more time with family or just having fun!

The amount of time saved depends on the software, the estimator, and the complexity of the jobs being estimated. As the estimator becomes more familiar with the system, efficiency improves and the time to do a given task decreases. The more complicated the job, the more the software can save you time by removing grunt work.

As a general rule, once you are proficient with the software, you should be able to complete a computerized estimate in 25 percent of the time that it will take you to do one manually.

Material Cost Control

Once the takeoff is complete and you have entered the quantities, you can easily generate a report of all the material required for the job. You can generate a summary, or a report broken down by job phase or type of materials.

You can then e-mail this to multiple suppliers to obtain competitive prices and fixed delivery dates. You can also share the estimate with a contractor's purchasing and accounting departments.

Cost tracking and inventory control become much simpler when you use software to generate and control the information. Material prices can be changed easily, quickly, and accurately at the last minute.

You can make information secure and easier to retrieve with various search criteria specific to what you are looking for.

You vastly reduce the investment in office space and filing cabinets, while reducing the fire fuel load that comes with storing large quantities of paper. But what if you do have a fire? A software-based system with remote backup means your information is safely out of harm's way.

A computer-based estimating system also provides for easy accumulation of project history that can be used to evaluate the accuracy of each new estimate.

Understanding Electrical Estimating | MikeHolt.com

Management

If integrated properly with the project management system, estimating software provides the flexibility to track projects in many ways, such as by system, floor, building, site, or project phase. A project manager can make a few mouse clicks to update the work breakdown structure, critical path, Gantt chart, and other key project management items in real time.

> A Gantt chart is a project management tool used primarily in the planning and scheduling of projects.

It is easy to share information with people in the field. Keeping the field supervisors apprised of the current labor budget, material information, and daily schedule updates help them complete work on time. The project manager can decide which reports to send out so people in the field are not overwhelmed by information they do not need.

Estimating software can also help supervisors in the field order material and better control its arrival at the jobsite. This reduces handling time, improves inventory control, reduces storage and theft problems, and assists with other issues that stem from inefficient material handling practices.

It is important to be sure an estimate is accurate and error free before using it for project management. Some companies require a re-estimate of a project after it is awarded.

Reduced Overhead

We have discussed the relatively high cost of producing a manual estimate and while this is a cost of doing business, controlling overhead is one of the core principles of making a higher profit.

A computer-based estimating system allows an estimator to bid on more jobs in the same amount of time, reducing estimating costs per bid relative to revenue. Material inventory control improves with accurate and available reports, providing such benefits as reduced costs for storage space and financing. You can also improve billing and expedite collections.

All of this will increase cash flow, which may further reduce your costs of capital and/or allow you to use your capital more effectively.

Confidence

A computer-assisted estimate provides increased confidence that the bid price is correct. It also provides more consistent and accurate historical data for future jobs of the same type. Tapping even a little of its potential will improve your competitiveness and increase your profit margins.

Purchase Considerations

Although many software vendors present information on the computer screen in a similar manner, you must think about the following during your consideration process:

Usability. Software should be logical, intuitive, simple to use, flexible, and easy to understand. It should provide an on-screen audit trail to review and modify the takeoff at any time.

Flexibility. It should provide the capability of factoring labor and/or material cost for every line of the takeoff to reflect diverse installation conditions. You should be able to view or change anything in the estimate at any point easily and quickly.

Reports. The system should provide a permanent audit trail that tracks the input. When looking at software options, pay close attention to the types of reports it will allow you to generate. You need reports that support your business processes. Determine what kinds of reports you need before you even look at estimating software.

Integration. Integration with your accounting system is important. Consider software that provides seamless integration, so you don't have to double-enter data.

Understanding Electrical Estimating | MikeHolt.com

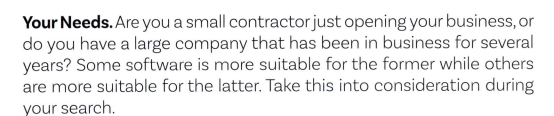

Your Needs. Are you a small contractor just opening your business, or do you have a large company that has been in business for several years? Some software is more suitable for the former while others are more suitable for the latter. Take this into consideration during your search.

Remember, you can always move up to a more sophisticated product when sales improve, sometimes with the same vendor. Only buy what you need.

Hardware Considerations

Do not make the mistake of trying to use an old, outdated computer to run new, super-charged software. Doing so will result in frustration and disappointment. Besides that, you will not receive the most from your investment.

How do you know if the hardware is outdated? If you are spending time waiting for the computer instead of getting work done, you need to upgrade.

If the computer is waiting on you instead of the other way around, then the fact that the computer is not very new may not matter. But, if you have an older computer, be sure the software you are considering will work with the operating system it uses.

Stay up to date with your hardware. Computers typically have a higher failure rate after two to three years of use. Purchase something that will handle the software you select without a lot of effort. There's nothing worse than listening to a loud computer fan screaming all day!

The software vendor you select can often suggest a good machine that meets their requirements.

Remember, "Time = Money." If you spend time waiting for the computer instead of working, you need to upgrade.

Understanding Electrical Estimating | Mike Holt Enterprises

Cost

It is tempting to save money on estimating software, rejecting anything over a certain price level. This kind of cost savings can actually be expensive in the long run. Instead, determine what your current and anticipated needs are, and then look at all of the software that meets those needs.

You need to consider all of the estimating software products, not just those with the lowest prices. The saying, "you get what you pay for" applies to software, too. If you have been on a jobsite after low-balling competitors have done the work, you understand all too well how this adage applies to electrical work.

Do not make the "low-price blindness" mistake in selecting your software. If it does not meet your needs, then the low-priced purchase is a waste of money.

The high-priced software purchase can also waste money. As you look at an increasing number of bells and whistles, you should evaluate those based on your present and anticipated future needs. Do some math to determine the return on investment of the added cost of an optional feature set or a more robust product.

With vendors that offer multiple versions or levels of estimating software, evaluate whether or not your data can migrate to an upgraded system later on, should you choose to purchase one of the lower-priced versions.

References

Before buying a computer-based estimating system, ask the vendor for a list of their users, then follow up by calling a few and asking how satisfied they are. Be sure to talk to at least one user who is similar in size to your company and does work similar to yours.

9.3 Backup System

Do not forget to have a backup system. There are many to choose from, but cloud-based solutions are probably your best bet for all-around ease of use and reliability.

9.4 Can I Afford It?

In today's world, it is highly unlikely you can be competitive if you estimate without the right software tools. The question is not whether you can afford the right system, but whether you can afford not to have adequate tools for estimating jobs in this competitive environment.

To determine the dollars required in sales to cover the purchase of estimating software, use the following formula:

Sales Increase Required per Year = Software Cost/Gross Profit Percent

Sales Increase to Cover Software Cost Example: How much must sales increase per year to cover the cost of an estimating system, based on the following factors? It includes software, computer, and training—$6,000; gross profit margin of 40 percent, with expected life of four years.

Sales = Cost per Year/Gross Profit Percent
Cost per Year = $6,000/4 years
Cost per Year = $1,500

Sales Required per Year = $1,500/40%
Sales Increase Required per Year = $3,750

Understanding Electrical Estimating | Mike Holt Enterprises

Smaller-Sized Contractor Income Statement Year Ending December 31		
Sales	$250,000	100% of Sales
Direct Job Cost		
Labor (4,000 Hrs)	$80,000	
Material	$70,000	
Total Direct Cost	$150,000	60% of Sales
Gross Profit	$100,000	40% of Sales
Overhead Expenses (Administrative Cost)		
Salaries and Commissions	$15,000	
Advertising	$5,000	
Auto and Gas	$10,000	
Benefits	$20,000	
Interest	$1,000	
Insurance—Auto, General, Workers' Comp.	$5,000	
Miscellaneous Expense	$3,000	
Payroll Taxes	$8,000	
Rent	$5,000	
Utilities/Phone	$3,000	
Total Administrative Expenses (50% of Prime)	$75,000	30% of Sales
Net Profit Before Taxes (16.67% of Prime)	$25,000	10% of Sales

9.5 Material Pricing Services

To use estimating software most effectively, you need to subscribe to a material pricing service to gain assurance you have the most current material prices. These programs interface with most major estimating software programs and can price almost all the individual material items in the database.

If you decide to use a pricing service:

- Verify that prices accurately reflect prices where your job is located
- Research reviews of the companies offering pricing services
- Ask where they obtain their material prices
- Find out their relationship to the electrical industry
- Get some references

Keep in mind that pricing services cannot keep up with the constantly changing conduit and wire prices, so you must check the prices for these items for each bid—especially when large quantities are included in the estimate.

Final Thoughts

Just as it takes time for an electrician to become a journeyman and then a master electrician, so it takes time to reach advanced levels of proficiency with estimating software.

How quickly you increase your proficiency depends on how good an estimator you already are and the amount of time you invest in learning the software. If you feel frustrated along the way, just relax and try to think through what the designer intended.

It is important to remember that estimating software is a tool and cannot by itself ensure your success. It allows estimators to improve accuracy, consistency, and speed when preparing estimates.

As you take what you have learned in the last nine chapters to the field and apply it, make sure to find some experienced mentors to give you advice when you approach new types of work and estimating challenges.

If you remember nothing else, make sure you stay away from the bad habit of chasing unprofitable work just so you can win. In the long run your goal is to make money and that should govern your entire estimating process.

Use the information you learned in this chapter to answer the following questions.

Chapter 9—Review Questions

9.1 Introduction

1. Estimating software cannot replace your ____ electrical installations or of the installation for which you are preparing an estimate.

    (a)   judgment in
    (b)   experience in
    (c)   knowledge of
    (d)   any of these

9.2 Estimating Software

2. There are a number of things to consider when learning about estimating software, so take your time as you review your needs for ____.

    (a)   bid analysis
    (b)   cost
    (c)   hardware
    (d)   all of these

3. Spreadsheets are appropriate for estimating ____.

    (a)   unit pricing
    (b)   change orders
    (c)   simple jobs
    (d)   all of these

Understanding Electrical Estimating | MikeHolt.com

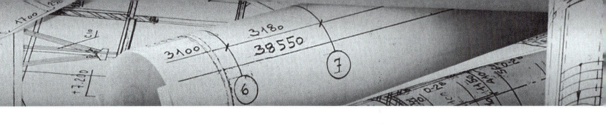

4. Some estimators will still use the manual takeoff to a paper system, and then enter the information into the ____.

(a) computer
(b) file folder
(c) calculator
(d) none of these

5. Most computer-based estimating supports ____.

(a) manual takeoffs
(b) direct takeoffs
(c) automatic on-screen takeoffs
(d) all of these

9.3 Backup System

6. There are many backup systems to choose from, but a(an) ____ is probably your best bet for all-around ease of use and reliability.

(a) external hard drive
(b) internal second hard drive
(c) cloud-based solution
(d) thumb drive

9.5 Material Pricing Services

7. To use estimating software most effectively, you need to subscribe to a ____ to gain assurance that you have the most current material prices.

(a) electrical products magazine
(b) electrical trades magazine
(c) material pricing service
(d) monthly price list

8. If you decide to use a pricing service, you should first ____.

(a) verify that prices accurately reflect prices where your job is located
(b) research reviews on companies offering pricing services
(c) find out their relationship to the electrical industry
(d) all of these

Notes...

Notes...

2nd Printing

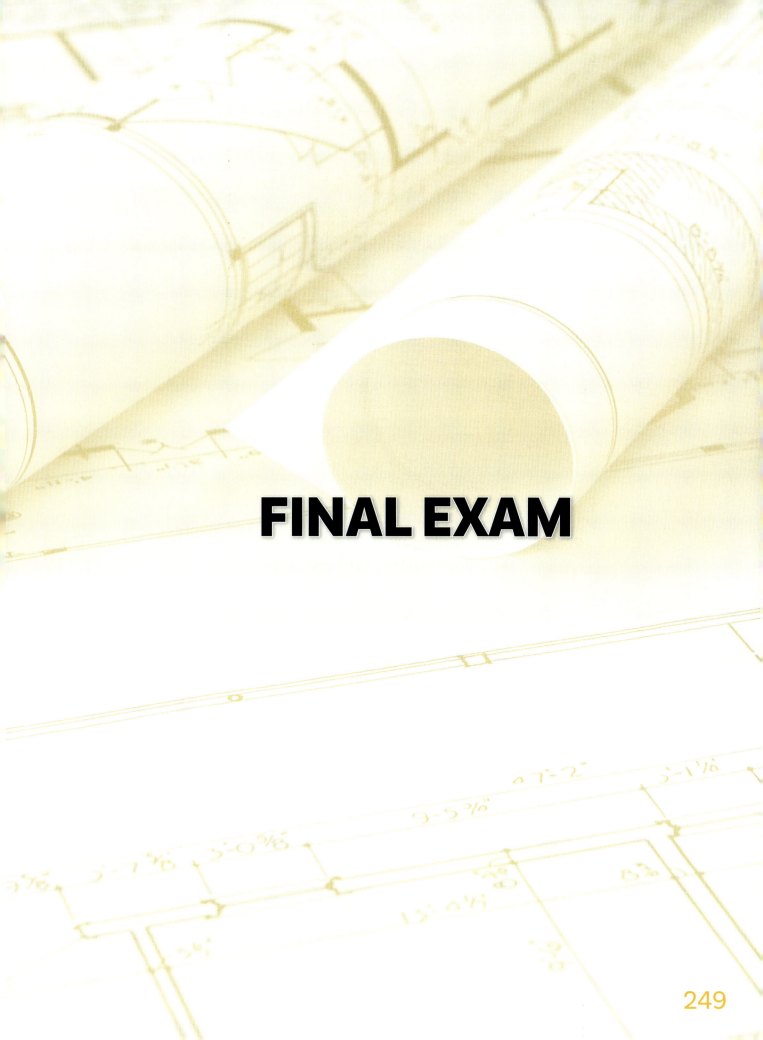

FINAL EXAM

Final Exam

1. The labor cost of any on the job training (OJT) due to your labor skill level, is your responsibility and those costs should ____.

    (a) be withheld from employee pay
    (b) not be passed on to your customers
    (c) be balanced out
    (d) be offset

2. When determining reasonable ____, consider the number of competitors who are expected to be bidding on the job and their experience in the particular line of work.

    (a) mark-up percentage
    (b) travel distance
    (c) profit margin
    (d) workforce

3. After you transfer the material cost from your price/labor worksheets to your estimate summary worksheet, the next step is to calculate total material costs accounting for ____.

    (a) miscellaneous material
    (b) tools
    (c) waste and theft
    (d) all of these

4. Once you have selected a software and before you start entering data, you need to ____.

(a) figure out how to pay for it
(b) evaluate it
(c) attend a seminar for it
(d) learn to use it

5. Material pricing services cannot keep up with ever-changing conduit and wire prices so you must check the prices for these items ____.

(a) daily
(b) weekly
(c) for each bid
(d) monthly

6. Once you have created the bill-of-material (BOM), it must be sent to your supplier(s) for ____.

(a) pricing
(b) review
(c) discounting
(d) product substitutions

7. Accurately estimated bids ____.

(a) result in work that you can handle
(b) provide opportunities to make money
(c) build rapport with your customers
(d) all of these

8. ____ is the bottom line. It is a report card against which all businesspersons are measured. A winning bid includes a reasonable amount for profit.

(a) Gross profit
(b) Net profit
(c) A comfortable retirement
(d) Success

Understanding Electrical Estimating | MikeHolt.com

9. Whatever takeoff system you use, be sure to use the same proce-dures every time, since consistency helps in reducing the time it takes to estimate a job, as well as _____.

   (a) reducing errors
   (b) increasing legibility
   (c) breaking even
   (d) reducing material waste

10. If you are using software to do an on-screen takeoff, make sure to use the same _____ used for a paper takeoff.

    (a) symbols
    (b) codes
    (c) designators
    (d) colors and system

11. As a part of being competitive remember that higher skilled elec-tricians earn the company more and _____.

    (a) should be paid more
    (b) are hard to find
    (c) are hard to replace
    (d) should get more time off

12. Most computer-based estimating supports _____.

    (a) manual takeoffs
    (b) direct takeoffs
    (c) automatic on-screen takeoffs
    (d) all of these

13. Information gathered from the takeoff is used to create the _____ required for the project.

    (a) initial order
    (b) material delivery schedule
    (c) anticipated completion date
    (d) bill-of-material (BOM)

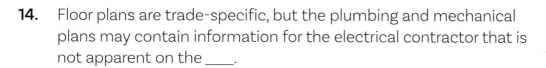

14. Floor plans are trade-specific, but the plumbing and mechanical plans may contain information for the electrical contractor that is not apparent on the ____.

    (a) civil plan
    (b) architectural plan
    (c) electrical floorplan
    (d) schematics

15. As a part of the overall bid process, an estimator needs to learn how to make an educated decision about when and where to spend our time and money to ____.

    (a) earn jobs
    (b) invest in equipment
    (c) hire employees
    (d) increase inventory

16. To develop and determine your own ____ adjustments, compare the estimated hours of a job against the actual number of hours it took.

    (a) assembly unit
    (b) composite unit
    (c) per-hundred units
    (d) labor-unit adjustments

17. As your annual business volume and revenue increase, the cost of overhead ____ decreases because it's split across more jobs.

    (a) per job
    (b) per item
    (c) per labor hour
    (d) for office space

Understanding Electrical Estimating | MikeHolt.com

18. You can look back at historical data to see what it took to complete a particular job (or aspect of a job) and make any ____ deemed necessary to labor units or material assemblies to ensure a more accurate bid.

    (a)   correlations
    (b)   adjustments
    (c)   deductions
    (d)   assessments

19. Unit pricing still requires a takeoff to determine the quantity of ____.

    (a)   boxes
    (b)   fittings
    (c)   each unit
    (d)   all of these

20. With unit pricing, ____ panelboards, communications cabinets, and so on, must still be measured in the usual manner due to the extreme variations between each one.

    (a)   smart wiring to
    (b)   homeruns to
    (c)   heights of
    (d)   space between

21. It does not help you to know the labor units your competitors use because ____ are unique to your company.

    (a)   your management style
    (b)   your organizational skills and weaknesses
    (c)   the skill of your labor force
    (d)   all of these

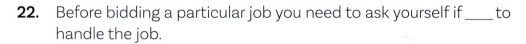

22. Before bidding a particular job you need to ask yourself if ____ to handle the job.

    (a) you have the financial resources
    (b) you have the proper tools and equipment
    (c) you have the workforce with the necessary skills
    (d) all of these

23. ____ provides a "feel" for what it takes to do a job. You should use personal experience to check your estimated labor requirements, and as a way to determine them.

    (a) Organizational experience
    (b) Company experience
    (c) Personal experience
    (d) Personnel experience

24. Whenever possible, purchase ____ or equipment that is installer-friendly.

    (a) refurbished equipment
    (b) preassembled equipment
    (c) recycled materials
    (d) less complicated equipment

25. High bids can cause you to lose the sales that your company depends on. Low bids can win sales but cause the ____.

    (a) loss of customers
    (b) loss of employees
    (c) loss of profits
    (d) loss of credibility

26. The ____ will assist in determining if any additional special labor and or equipment might be needed to install your equipment and fixtures.

    (a) civil plans
    (b) architectural plans
    (c) site plans
    (d) schematics

27. When calculating labor, many electrical contractors estimate a job based on how long they think it will take them ____.

    (a) to get to the worksite
    (b) to get paid
    (c) to do it
    (d) to train the staff

28. There is nothing wrong with telling a potential customer that you don't wish to bid on a job, especially if there is ____.

    (a) a lack of civility
    (b) an unsafe work environment
    (c) unethical behavior
    (d) any of these

29. Smaller jobs require ____ because there is the same base costs as a large job without the volume of work to offset the costs.

    (a) a much higher mark-up
    (b) a much higher overhead
    (c) a much higher labor unit
    (d) the same number of workers

30. Determining labor costs consists of looking up the labor unit associated with each ____ and entering those values on the Price/Labor Worksheet.

    (a) material item
    (b) function
    (c) installation
    (d) assembly

31. Additional labor requirements for the ____ for the job are not adjustments of the labor unit for job conditions, but additional labor that might be required.

    (a) selling price
    (b) net cost
    (c) mark-up percentage
    (d) break-even cost

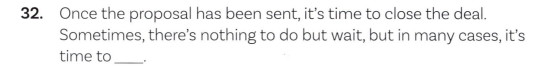

32. Once the proposal has been sent, it's time to close the deal. Sometimes, there's nothing to do but wait, but in many cases, it's time to ____.

(a) move on
(b) touch base with the customer
(c) review your proposal
(d) re-submit your proposal

33. Another common estimating method is to perform a "Guestimate" and "look at the job" to decide what it's worth based on what someone remembers about a type of job and how it feels based on ____.

(a) common knowledge
(b) common sense
(c) material costs
(d) past experiences

34. Architectural drawings will include information such as building and structural materials, wall cross-sections and dimensions, wall and floor finishes, and ____.

(a) elevator locations
(b) building elevations
(c) emergency egress
(d) job trailer locations

35. Once the takeoff is complete, the next step is to determine the bill of material which means determining the ____ of all material items..

(a) type
(b) size
(c) quantity
(d) all of these

36. Extreme temperatures causes workers to become distracted which can result in ____.

    (a) more accidents
    (b) deterioration in workmanship
    (c) lower productivity
    (d) all of these

37. Another part of being competitive is when considering ____, do not pick up your material if you have the option of having it delivered as it costs more to pick it up.

    (a) profits
    (b) material costs
    (c) discounts
    (d) mark-up

38. It is difficult to cope with last minute changes to the drawings or specifications if you have to recalculate ____.

    (a) a manual estimate
    (b) travel distance
    (c) a computer-assisted estimate
    (d) a bill of materials

39. The two basic choices when selecting estimating software: a spreadsheet or a software suite. Spreadsheets are appropriate if ____.

    (a) you don't bid on larger jobs
    (b) don't have the money to invest in a software suite
    (c) don't have the required skillset
    (d) don't have the office space

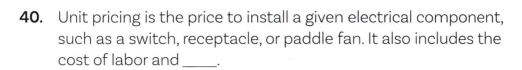

40. Unit pricing is the price to install a given electrical component, such as a switch, receptacle, or paddle fan. It also includes the cost of labor and _____.

(a) material
(b) overhead
(c) profit
(d) all of these

41. _____, for a contracting company, exists in the records of past jobs. If they are like the one you are estimating, you can carry over much of the information to the new job.

(a) Organizational experience
(b) Company experience
(c) Personal experience
(d) Personnel experience

42. Once you have some old-work experience and job history, you will be better prepared to adjust the labor for future projects. But _____ labor unit for fishing and cutting in boxes is not a bad place to start.

(a) doubling the
(b) tripling the
(c) adding 25 percent to the
(d) adding 50 percent to the

43. Indirect costs include _____.

(a) employee benefits
(b) business operational overhead
(c) management expenses
(d) all of these

Understanding Electrical Estimating | MikeHolt.com

44. Because unit pricing is faster and easier than detailed estimating, it takes less time and costs your company less money to determine the ____ for a job.

    (a) selling price
    (b) scheduling
    (c) manpower
    (d) lead time

45. Estimating software can help improve accuracy quite a bit, particularly during the ____ of your estimates.

    (a) extension phase
    (b) takeoff phase
    (c) material costs calculations
    (d) labor costs calculations

46. If you get a bad feeling in your gut when you are in communication with a potential customer, you should trust your instincts and don't allow ____ to override that feeling in your gut.

    (a) arrogance
    (b) over-confidence
    (c) ego
    (d) greed

47. ____ drawings are the final stage of design drawings.

    (a) Schematic
    (b) Design
    (c) Construction
    (d) One-Line

48. Your project management team needs to know what the ____ is and to assign tasks to your employees that they like to do and at which they excel.

    (a) labor budget
    (b) schedule
    (c) bid price
    (d) total job cost

49. Most contractors apply overhead as a percentage of ____.

    (a) labor budget
    (b) prime cost
    (c) material costs
    (d) selling price

50. You can remain competitive if you remember that when it comes to your ____, confidence and professionalism are important ingredients in getting your price.

    (a) bottom-line
    (b) success
    (c) selling price
    (d) attitude

51. When determining a job's break-even-point, the first step is to transfer the totals for ____ to a summary worksheet.

    (a) permit fees
    (b) sales tax
    (c) labor hours and material costs
    (d) consulting fees

52. The labor rate hour contributing to your break-even-cost can be determined by ____.

    (a) The Bureau of Labor Statistics
    (b) local and national averages
    (c) shop and job averages
    (d) prevailing wage rates

53. Consider the financial effect of a job before you bid it. If you can't financially manage it, then ____.

    (a) verify your lines of credit
    (b) seek out a construction loan
    (c) don't bid it
    (d) collaborate with another contractor

Understanding Electrical Estimating | MikeHolt.com

54. The estimate summary worksheet has ____ major sections.

    (a) four
    (b) five
    (c) six
    (d) seven

55. The layout of the work represents ____ of the labor unit.

    (a) 15 percent
    (b) 12.5 percent
    (c) 25 percent
    (d) 50 percent

56. An accurate estimate relies on ____ for every detail.

    (a) accounting
    (b) price lists
    (c) books
    (d) product samples

57. Typical site considerations to be used for the purposes of estimating using labor unit include that ____ equipment is supplied by others.

    (a) high-reach
    (b) lift
    (c) excavation
    (d) all of these

58. The scope of work describes the work that needs to be done ____.

    (a) for a project
    (b) within a certain time frame
    (c) in house
    (d) by subcontractors

59. Other considerations that can have an effect on labor units are ____.

    (a) having qualified personnel
    (b) your attitude and staff motivation
    (c) employee training
    (d) all of these

60. Performing a takeoff one page of the drawings at a time, or takeoff the wiring for the first floor, then all of the wiring for the second floor, and so on describes the ____ system.

    (a) Section-at-a-Time
    (b) Beginning-to-End
    (c) End-to-Beginning
    (d) Long Method

61. When performing a percentage of distribution check, check the percentage distribution of ____ relative to sales.

    (a) labor, material, direct job cost
    (b) overhead
    (c) profit
    (d) all of these

62. Once you have created the bill-of-material (BOM), it must be sent to your supplier(s) for ____.

    (a) pricing
    (b) review
    (c) discounting
    (d) product substitutions

63. Shrinkage is a term often used to describe the effects of waste and theft of material on the jobsite. For an efficiently managed job, ____ is reasonable.

    (a) two percent
    (b) three percent
    (c) four percent
    (d) five percent

Understanding Electrical Estimating | MikeHolt.com

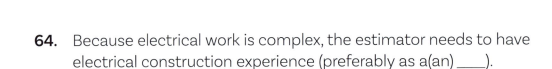

64. Because electrical work is complex, the estimator needs to have electrical construction experience (preferably as a(an) ____).

   (a) electrician
   (b) apprentice electrician
   (c) journeyman electrician
   (d) master electrician

65. The design drawing stage(s) is(are) the ____ drawings.

   (a) schematic
   (b) design development
   (c) construction
   (d) all of these

66. Before submitting your bid to the customer, do as much bid analysis as possible to ensure your price is as ____ as possible and nothing falls through the cracks.

   (a) profitable
   (b) accurate
   (c) risk-free
   (d) appealing

67. Most electrical contractors are concerned about their ability to ____, make money, and stay in business.

   (a) be competitive
   (b) be financially independent
   (c) work from the home or office
   (d) take time off

68. The final step in the detailed estimate process is to ____.

   (a) apply overhead and profit
   (b) perform a bid analysis
   (c) submit the proposal
   (d) apply your license seal

69. Information gathered from the takeoff is used to create the _____ required for the project.

     (a) initial order
     (b) material delivery schedule
     (c) anticipated completion date
     (d) bill-of-material (BOM)

70. Material handling and cleanup represents _____ of the labor unit.

     (a) 10 percent
     (b) 12.5 percent
     (c) 25 percent
     (d) 50 percent

71. The purpose of counting symbols during takeoff is to determine the _____ of a given electrical component or assembly that will be required on the job.

     (a) type
     (b) size
     (c) rating
     (d) quantity

72. Increased bid accuracy is one advantage of using estimating software as errors with pricing material and the application of labor units will be _____.

     (a) non-existent
     (b) tolerable
     (c) significantly reduced
     (d) more profitable

73. Large high-resolution monitors are a great help when working on spreadsheets, digital plans, or _____.

     (a) meeting notes
     (b) project documentation
     (c) email
     (d) codes materials

Understanding Electrical Estimating | MikeHolt.com

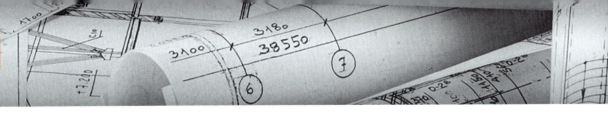

74. You can safely use unit pricing on ____.

    (a) renovations
    (b) change orders
    (c) small scope jobs
    (d) all of these

75. Many electricians feel obligated to bid a job, even when it is not likely to be profitable. If you don't think you are going to make money on the job, ____.

    (a) over bid it to compensate in case you get the job
    (b) better to lose money than a customer
    (c) don't bid on it
    (d) try to negotiate

Notes...

Notes...

THE MIKE HOLT TEAM

ABOUT THE AUTHOR

Mike Holt
Founder and President
Mike Holt Enterprises
Groveland, Florida

Mike Holt is an author, businessman, educator, speaker, publisher and *National Electrical Code* expert. He has written hundreds of electrical training books and articles, founded three successful businesses, and has taught thousands of electrical *Code* seminars across the U.S. and internationally. His dynamic presentation style, deep understanding of the trade, and ability to connect with students are some of the reasons that he is one of the most sought-after speakers in the industry.

His company, Mike Holt Enterprises, has been serving the electrical industry for over 50 years, with a commitment to creating and publishing books, videos, online training, and curriculum support for electrical trainers, students, organizations, and electrical professionals. His devotion to the trade, coupled with the lessons he learned at the University of Miami's MBA program, have helped him build one of the largest electrical training and publishing companies in the United States.

Mike is committed to changing lives and helping people take their careers to the next level. He has always felt a responsibility to provide education beyond the scope of just passing an exam. He draws on his previous experience as an electrician, inspector, contractor and instructor, to guide him in developing powerful training solutions that electricians understand and enjoy. He is always mindful of how hard learning can be for students who are intimidated by school, by their feelings towards learning, or by the complexity of the *NEC*. He's mastered the art of simplifying and clarifying complicated technical concepts and his extensive use of illustrations helps students apply the content and relate the material to their work in the field. His ability to take the intimidation out of learning is reflected in the successful careers of his students.

Mike's commitment to pushing boundaries and setting high standards extends into his personal life as well. He's an eight-time Overall National Barefoot Waterski Champion. Mike has more than 20 gold medals, many national records, and has competed in three World Barefoot Tournaments. In 2015, at the tender age of 64, he started a new adventure—competitive mountain bike racing and at 65 began downhill mountain biking. Every day he continues to find ways to motivate himself, both mentally and physically.

Mike and his wife, Linda, reside in New Mexico and Florida, and are the parents of seven children and eight grandchildren. As his life has changed over the years, a few things have remained constant: his commitment to God, his love for his family, and doing what he can to change the lives of others through his products and seminars.

Special Acknowledgments

My Family. First, I want to thank God for my godly wife who's always by my side and for my children.

My Staff. A personal thank you goes to my team at Mike Holt Enterprises for all the work they do to help me with my mission of changing peoples' lives through education. They work tirelessly to ensure that, in addition to our products meeting and exceeding the educational needs of our customers, we stay committed to building life-long relationships throughout their electrical careers.

ABOUT THE ILLUSTRATOR

Mike Culbreath—Illustrator
Graphic Illustrator
Alden, Michigan

Mike Culbreath has devoted his career to the electrical industry and worked his way up from apprentice electrician to master electrician. He started working in the electrical field doing residential and light commercial construction, and later did service work and custom electrical installations. While working as a journeyman electrician, he suffered a serious on-the-job knee injury. As part of his rehabilitation, Mike completed courses at Mike Holt Enterprises, and then passed the exam to receive his Master Electrician's license. In 1986, with a keen interest in continuing education for electricians, he joined the staff to update material and began illustrating Mike Holt's textbooks and magazine articles.

Mike started with simple hand-drawn diagrams and cut-and-paste graphics. Frustrated by the limitations of that style of illustrating, he took a company computer home to learn how to operate some basic computer graphics software. Realizing that computer graphics offered a lot of flexibility for creating illustrations, Mike took every computer graphics class and seminar he could to help develop his skills. He worked as an illustrator and editor with the company for over 30 years and, as Mike Holt has proudly acknowledged, has helped to transform his words and visions into lifelike graphics.

Mike, retired in 2020 and now lives in northern lower Michigan where he enjoys hiking, kayaking, photography, gardening, and cooking; but his real passion is his horses. He also loves spending time with his children Dawn and Mac and his grandchildren Jonah, Kieley, and Scarlet.

ABOUT THE MIKE HOLT TEAM

There are many people who played a role in the production of this textbook. Their efforts are reflected in the quality and organization of the information contained in this textbook, and in its technical accuracy, completeness, and usability.

The Content Team

Daniel Brian House
Vice President of Digital and Technical Training
Mike Holt Enterprises, Instructor, Master Electrician
Ocala, Florida

Brian House is Vice President of Digital and Technical Training at Mike Holt Enterprises, and a Certified Mike Holt Instructor. He is a permanent member of the video teams, on which he has served since the 2011 *Code* cycle. Brian has worked in the trade since the 1990s in residential, commercial and industrial settings. He opened a contracting firm in 2003 that designed energy-efficient lighting retrofits, explored "green" biomass generators, and partnered with residential PV companies in addition to traditional electrical installation and service.

In 2007, Brian was personally selected by Mike for development and began teaching seminars for Mike Holt Enterprises after being named a "Top Gun Presenter" in Mike's Train the Trainer boot camp. Brian travels around the country teaching electricians, instructors,

Understanding Electrical Estimating | MikeHolt.com

military personnel, and engineers. His experience in the trenches as an electrical contractor, along with Mike Holt's instructor training, gives him a teaching style that is practical, straightforward, and refreshing.

Today, as Vice President of Digital and Technical Training at Mike Holt Enterprises, Brian leads the apprenticeship and digital product teams. They create cutting-edge training tools, and partner with in-house and apprenticeship training programs nationwide to help them reach the next level. He is also part of the content team that helps Mike bring his products to market, assisting in the editing of the textbooks, coordinating the content and illustrations, and assuring the technical accuracy and flow of the information.

Brian served as the chief editor for this new edition of Understanding Electrical Estimating and assembled the team for the video production, and content review of this textbook and its supporting resources.

Brian is high energy, with a passion for doing business the right way. He expresses his commitment to the industry and his love for its people in his teaching, working on books, and developing instructional programs and software tools.

Brian and his wife Carissa have shared the joy of their four children and many foster children during 25 years of marriage. When not mentoring youth at work or church, he can be found racing mountain bikes or SCUBA diving with his kids. He's passionate about helping others and regularly engages with the youth of his community to motivate them into exploring their future.

Mario Valdes
Technical Content Editor, Electrical Inspector,
Electrical Plans Examiner, Master Electrician
Ocala, Florida

Mario Valdes, Jr. is a member of the technical team at Mike Holt Enterprises, working directly with Mike Holt in researching, re-writing, and coordinating content, to ensure that it is technically accurate, relatable, and valuable to all electrical professionals. He plays an important role in gathering research, analyzing data, and assisting

Mike in the writing of the textbooks. He reworks content into different formats to improve the flow of information and to ensure expectations are being met in terms of message, tone, and quality. He edits illustrations and proofreads content to "fact-check" each sentence, title, and image structure. Mario enjoys working in collaboration with Mike and Brian to enhance the company's brand image, training products, and technical publications.

Mario is a permanent member of the video teams, on which he has served since the 2017 *Code* cycle.

Mario is licensed as an Electrical Contractor, most recently having worked as an electrical inspector and plans examiner for an engineering firm in South Florida. Additionally, he was an Electrical Instructor for a technical college, teaching students pursuing an associate degree in electricity. He taught subjects such as ac/dc fundamentals, residential and commercial wiring, blueprint reading, and electrical estimating. He brings to the Mike Holt team a wealth of knowledge and devotion for the *NEC*.

He started his career at 16 years old in his father's electrical contracting company. Once he got his Florida State contractor's license, he ran the company as project manager and estimator. Mario's passion for the *NEC* prompted him to get his inspector and plans review certifications and embark on a new journey in electrical *Code* compliance. He's worked on complex projects such as hospitals, casinos, hotels and multi-family high rise buildings. Mario is very passionate about educating electrical professionals about electrical safety and the *National Electrical Code*.

Mario's a member of the IAEI, NFPA, and ICC, and enjoys participating in the meetings; he believes that by staying active in these organizations he'll be ahead of the game, with cutting-edge knowledge pertaining to safety codes.

When not immersed in the electrical world Mario enjoys fitness training. He resides in Pembroke Pines, Florida with his beautiful family, which includes his wife and his three sons. They enjoy family trip getaways to Disney World and other amusement parks.

Understanding Electrical Estimating | MikeHolt.com

Editorial and Production

Toni Culbreath has served as a copy editor for decades at Mike Holt Enterprises. Her tireless efforts to proofread and edit our many publications and attention to detail are present in many of our publications.

Cathleen Kwas handled the design, layout, and typesetting of this book. Her desire to create the best possible product for our customers is greatly appreciated, and she constantly pushes the design envelope to make the product experience just a little bit better.

Vinny Perez and **Eddie Anacleto** have been a dynamic team. They have taken the best instructional graphics in the industry to the next level. Both Eddie and Vinny bring years of graphic art experience to the pages of this book and have been a huge help updating and improving the content, look, and style our graphics.

Dan Haruch is an integral part of the video recording process and spends much of his time making sure that the instructor resources created from this product are the best in the business. His dedication to the instructor and student experience is much appreciated.

John Donahue and **Donahue Architecture, Inc.** A special thanks to John and the staff at Donahue Architecture, Inc., who graciously allowed the use of their architectural plans used throughout this program.

Kevin Drawdy, quotations specialist at City Electric Supply in Maitland, Florida, donated his time to be with the team for the recording process. His contribution as it relates to cost of material and relationships with supply houses was greatly appreciated.

Additional Video Team Members

The following special people provided technical advice in the development of this textbook as they served on the video team.

Boyd Bindrup
Electrical Contractor/Instructor
Ogden, UT

Boyd Bindrup launched his electrical career at age 12 by working for his father's company during the summers and earning $0.75 per hr. He began his electrical apprenticeship in Ogden Weber Technical College, but left to attend Salt Lake Community College for his last two years of training. After finishing school, he obtained his Journeyman license and, two years later, his Master Electrician license. He later returned to Ogden Weber Tech and has been an instructor there teaching Electrical Apprentices since 1994.

Boyd is an Electrical Contractor license holder for Creative Times, Inc. (CTI Electric) which does primarily commercial and military electrical work. He has been teaching continuing education classes for over 20 years having taught over 2,000 classes, and trained thousands of electricians.

He's a Utah, Idaho and Colorado Master Electrician, and his credentials include LEED AP BD+C, Lightning Protection Master Installer/Designer, Vindicator Certified Security Installer, Cathodic Protection Installer CP1 NACE 56675, Fiber Optics Installer #FOIUT216, and SKM Arc Flash Power Tools trained.

Boyd is devoted to learning and passing on the knowledge to current and future electrical professionals. He is passionate about the direction of the profession and is active politically in the industry.

Boyd and his wife Rebecca reside in Ogden Canyon Utah and are parents to six children. His hobbies include CrossFit, Mountain biking, and Xterra triathlon.

Understanding Electrical Estimating | MikeHolt.com

Ryan Carlson
Director of Digital Training
Ocala, Florida

Ryan Carlson currently serves as the Director of Digital Training for Mike Holt Enterprises. He is the "go-to" Capacitor specialist, providing support for schools, instructors, and contractors to get the most from the Capacitor and apprenticeship. As a member of the apprenticeship team, he manages the online apprenticeship content, uploading new content, and updating existing content. He is also a Mike Holt Certified Instructor, and manages the team of programmers and software engineers that develop and keep the system running.

Ryan grew up on a small family farm and worked in both the construction and agriculture industries to pay his way through college. He holds a bachelor's degree in business administration with an accounting minor and is a journeyman electrician in the State of Florida.

Starting as a "romex jockey" while in high school, Ryan has worked in many different areas of the electrical field. After graduating college, he worked in the office of an electrical contractor, filling roles from dispatcher to Accounts Receivable and Accounts Payable.

Missing the field action, Ryan moved back into the field where he got his Journeyman license and became a Senior Field Technician, overseeing crews and jobs of various sizes.

Out in the literal trenches, his specialty was service work, troubleshooting, and dealing with distressed customers. His area of work was varied, including residential and mobile homes, commercial restaurants, industrial aggregate plants, and healthcare. As a Generac-certified technician in Florida, he has installed and maintained countless generators.

Ryan currently lives in Florida with his wife and two children. When he isn't helping MHE instructors, you will find him with his family enjoying trips to the Smokey Mountains.

Jim Glass
District Manager
City Electric Supply, Deland, Florida

Jim Glass began his career in Electrical Distribution in 1977, working for Graybar Electric in St. Petersburg, Florida at the young age of 16. He started in the warehouse, and over the years worked his way up to inside sales.

In 1986 he was promoted to sub-branch supervisor in Naples, Florida, and the following year was offered an outside sales position, which is the position he was in when his 18-year tenure with Graybar ended. From there he moved to Ocala, Florida and took a position with Marin Bochner Inc., a large electrical manufacturer's agency, as a sales representative.

In 1997, the opportunity that changed Jim's life, and set his career into orbit, came when he was offered a job managing the local branch in Ocala for City Electric Supply. He spent three years managing the Ocala branch, and in 2000 was promoted to District Manager of the Orlando District over eight stores. In 2006 he was offered the opportunity to move with his family to Ohio to pioneer a new market for the company. He was promoted to Regional Manager, and over the next three years opened 16 branches in the Ohio market. In 2009 during the Great Recession, he was asked to take on additional responsibilities, and took over the Chicago market consisting of 32 branches.

In 2017, Jim came back to Florida with the company as a District Manager in the Orlando and Daytona Beach markets. He just celebrated his 26th year with City Electric Supply!

Jim has been married to his wife Andrea for 31 years and they have two sons; Justin, who is a Marine special forces Staff Sergeant; and Javey who is also in the electrical industry working for ESI in Tampa as an Outside Sales Rep. In their spare time they love to travel, as well as spend time in the outdoors boating, fishing, and hunting.

Understanding Electrical Estimating | MikeHolt.com

Paul Heard
Authers Building Group
Prosper, Texas

Paul Heard was born and educated in southern England. He went to secondary education with the London Institute of Technology, while working for a local general contractor in the commercial and industrial sector. After three years teaching in the Bournemouth and Poole College of Further Education, he took the opportunity to work in continental Europe, and moved back to London towards the end of the 1990s.

In 2000 Paul moved to the U.S. for a Project Management job in Ohio. Initially involved in the management of design and build projects, he soon started estimating on a variety of projects, some of which he took through construction and final completion. He has estimated projects ranging from retail through multi-family, offices, schools, municipal facilities, high-rise and hospitals, from $100,000 to $300,000,000. The Christchurch earthquake of 2010 took him to New Zealand to take the lead estimating role in rebuilding projects.

In 2015 he returned to the U.S. and located in Dallas, Texas. Now the Chief Estimator for Authers Building Group, he is engaged in school, higher education, and commercial work of both the preconstruction, design and build, as well as competitive sealed proposal procurement delivery systems. Very much a general contractor, and having worked for a subcontractor, he understands the experience from the "other side," and he has a view of the full range of the industry with this experience-national and international, project management, subcontractor, general contractor, preconstruction, and estimating.

Paul has three beautiful daughters who have a variety of interests. He always refers to himself as boring-he enjoys reading and walking! Paul also likes watching cricket, although when younger, playing the game was very much a favorite pastime. He also enjoys Formula1 motor racing and rugby union.

Richard Jaffarian
Electrical Resources, Inc.
Titusville, Florida

Richard Jaffarian is the president of Electrical Resources, Inc. which he founded in 1975. He began his career in 1968 as an electrical engineer with a consulting engineering firm. In 1971, he was the vice president of his family-owned electrical contracting firm with an annual volume of $20M.

Richard introduced his first estimating software program in 1976 to efficiently meet his clients demands in a timely fashion while maintaining complete and accurate bills of material. The diversity of the more than 31,000 projects he has been involved in has allowed him to build what is now recognized as the most complete and comprehensive estimating database in the electrical industry. His current estimating software suite includes On-Screen Takeoff, AutoBranch, Auto Duct Bank, Auto Fire Alarm, Request for Quotes, Purchase Orders and T&M Billing.

Richard developed the Quantum Professional Estimating Suite and LinkPricer that provides current contractor-level pricing for third-party estimating software. His established contacts and accounts allow him to publish and update material prices at the contractor level, and are recognized as the most realistic material prices in the industry.

Richard is the author and publisher of Electrical Estimating Tips and Techniques, the Electrical Labor Units Manual, the National Electrical Price Guide, and the On-Line Electrical Price and Labor Units Guide. He is qualified to testify as an expert witness regarding electrical plans, specifications, estimates, change orders, material pricing, and labor units. He also teaches estimating, how to determine the volume of estimating required to meet overhead and profit goals, and how actual volume plays an important role in varying the overhead and profit mark-ups.

Understanding Electrical Estimating | MikeHolt.com

Eric Stromberg, P.E.
Electrical Engineer, Instructor
Los Alamos, New Mexico

Eric Stromberg has a bachelor's degree in Electrical Engineering and is a professional engineer. He started in the electrical industry when he was a teenager helping the neighborhood electrician. After high school, and a year of college, Eric worked for a couple of different audio companies, installing sound systems in a variety of locations from small buildings to baseball stadiums. After returning to college, he worked as a journeyman wireman for an electrical contractor.

After graduating from the University of Houston, Eric took a job as an electronic technician and installed and serviced life safety systems in high-rise buildings. After seven years he went to work for Dow Chemical as a power distribution engineer. His work with audio systems had made him very sensitive to grounding issues and he took this experience with him into power distribution. Because of this expertise, Eric became one of Dow's grounding subject matter experts. This is also how Eric met Mike Holt, as Mike was looking for grounding experts for his 2002 Grounding vs. Bonding video.

Eric taught the *National Electrical Code* for professional engineering exam preparation for over 20 years, and has held continuing education teacher certificates for the states of Texas and New Mexico. He was on the electrical licensing and advisory board for the State of Texas, as well as on their electrician licensing exam board.

Eric now consults for a Department of Energy research laboratory in New Mexico, where he's responsible for the electrical standards as well as assisting the laboratory's AHJ.

Eric's oldest daughter lives with her husband in Zurich, Switzerland, where she teaches for an international school. His son served in the Air Force, has a degree in Aviation logistics, and is a pilot and owner of an aerial photography business. His youngest daughter is a singer/songwriter in Los Angeles.